1923 An Equal Rights Amendment, drafted by the National Woman's Party founder Alice Paul, is first introduced in Congress. The legislation says, "Men and women shall have equal rights throughout the United States and every place subject to its jurisdiction." Kodak introduces home movie equipment. A vaccine is developed for whooping cough. George Burns and Gracie Allen form a comedy team.

1924 Nellie Taylor Ross of Wyoming is the first woman elected governor of a state. Congress grants Native Americans U.S. citizenship.

1925 AT&T offers the first commercial fax service in America.

1926 Bertha Knight Landes is elected mayor of Seattle. She is the first woman elected mayor of a sizable city. The first electric steam irons go on sale.

1927 *The Jazz Singer*, starring Al Jolson, is the first popular "talkie." Clara Bow becomes the "It Girl" in the movie *It*. Charles Lindbergh makes the first solo transatlantic flight. Babe Ruth hits sixty home runs in one season. Homogenized milk is introduced.

1928 Two million people attend vaudeville shows daily. *Plane Crazy*, Walt Disney's first cartoon featuring Mickey Mouse, is released. The first annual Academy Awards are held; Janet Gaynor wins for Best Actress, Emil Jannings wins for Best Actor. *Amos and Andy* begins broadcasting, and becomes the longest running radio series in history. Joseph Stalin becomes the leader of the Soviet Union. Sir Alexander Fleming observes the antibiotic properties of the penicillin mold.

1929 The stock market crashes in October, sending the country into a depression that will last through the next decade.

1930 Jean Harlow is the "Blonde Bombshell" in *Hell's Angels*. The motion picture industry voluntarily adopts standards of good taste in motion pictures. Pluto is discovered. The modern gas turbine is developed, leading directly to the jet engine. Sliced bread becomes available. The first supermarket opens on Long Island, New York.

1931 The 102-floor Empire State Building is completed. Women make up about 44 percent of college students. Bing Crosby stars in his own radio show and his records begin selling by the millions. Pearl Buck wins a Pulitzer Prize for *The Good Earth*.

1932 Amelia Earhart makes a solo flight across the Atlantic. John and Lionel Barrymore, Greta Garbo, and Joan Crawford star in *Grand Hotel*. *The Ed Sullivan Show*, *The Jack Benny Show*, *The Shadow*, and *Buck Rogers* are all new to radio. Franklin D. Roosevelt is elected president, promising a "new deal."

1933 Frances Perkins is appointed Secretary of Labor, making her the first woman in a presidential cabinet. The National Industrial Recovery Act forbids more than one family member to hold a government job; three-fourths of those forced from their jobs are women. Hitler becomes chancellor of Germany. Prohibition ends.

1934 Shirley Temple, age six, makes her first full-length film and wins a special Oscar as "outstanding personality of 1934." Benny Goodman forms his own twelve-piece band, introducing the "swing era." Crime duo Bonnie and Clyde are gunned down near Gibsland, Louisiana.

1935 The Social Security Act is signed into law. The Supreme Court declares the NIRA unconstitutional. Two months later Congress enacts the National Labor Relations Act, providing even stronger government support for organized labor. Italy invades Ethiopia. Nylon is created.

1936 Eleanor Roosevelt begins writing her column, "My Day," which is syndicated in sixty newspapers. *The Milton Berle Show* premieres on radio. Margaret Mitchell's *Gone With the Wind* is published. Hitler exhibits Nazi propaganda at the Berlin Olympics.

1937 The American Medical Association recognizes birth control as an integral part of medical practice and education. *The Guiding Light* soap opera premieres on radio. Amelia Earhart disappears while attempting to fly around the world. The Xerox copying method is invented.

1938 A new U.S. Food, Drug, and Cosmetic Act requires drug manufacturers to test products for safety and efficacy before putting them on the market. Germany annexes Austria and parts of Czechoslovakia. Orson Welles broadcasts his "War of the Worlds." Roy Rogers's singing cowboy career is launched with the release of *Under Western Stars*. *Snow White* is the first feature-length animated cartoon. Irving Berlin's "God Bless America" becomes a popular hit.

1939 Television is introduced at the New York World's Fair. Hattie McDaniel is the first African-American woman to win an Academy Award, for her role as Mammy in *Gone With the Wind*. "Over the Rainbow," from *The Wizard of Oz*, wins the award for best song, and Judy Garland receives a special Oscar as "the best juvenile performer of the year." Bra-cup sizing is developed in the United States. World War II begins September 1, as German troops invade Poland. Polish Jews are forced into ghettos.

1940 The first nylon stockings go on sale. Mae West cowrites and costars with W. C. Fields in *My Little Chickadee*. The Republican Party comes out in support of the Equal Rights Amendment.

1941 Germany invades the Soviet Union. Japan bombs Pearl Harbor. The House of Representatives votes 388 to 1 to approve a war resolution against Japan; as in the World War I vote, Representative Rankin casts the only dissenting vote. The United States also declares war on Italy and Germany. Women are encouraged to take jobs during the war; Rosie the Riveter becomes a national symbol.

1942 The Women's Army Auxiliary Corps is established to use women in noncombat positions to free more men to fight. President Roosevelt authorizes the internment of more than 110,000 persons of Japanese ancestry living in the United States. The Manhattan Project is created to produce the first atomic bomb. The Nazis implement their "Final Solution," the systematic extermination of all Jews in Europe. Frank Sinatra plays New York's Paramount Theatre.

1943 Rubber, metal, paper, silk, and nylon are collected for recycling. Flour, fish, meat, canned foods, and shoes are all rationed. Germany occupies Italy. Fox Studios insures Betty Grable's legs for a million dollars. The All-American Girls Professional Baseball League is founded.

1944 Harvard University's Mark I is the first general-purpose digital computer. Allied invasion forces land in Normandy on June 6 (D-Day). FDR wins a fourth term as president. Penicillin is mass-produced. The Democratic Party endorses the Equal Rights Amendment. "Queen of the Surf" Esther Williams becomes a star in *Bathing Beauty*. Elizabeth Taylor and Mickey Rooney star in *National Velvet*.

1945 Allied forces liberate concentration camps. Atomic bombs are dropped on Hiroshima and Nagasaki. World War II ends, having taken 55 million lives worldwide. A total of 350,000 women have served in the U.S. military during the war. The United Nations is created and Eleanor Roosevelt becomes a delegate. Although many women lose their jobs as servicemen return from the war, the number of women in the workforce will never again fall as low as prewar levels.

WE REMEMBER

WE REMEMBER

Women Born at the Turn of the Century Tell the Stories of Their Lives

in Words and Pictures

Jeanne Marie Laskas

Photographs by Lynn Johnson

William Morrow and Company, Inc.

New York

Photographs on the following pages by Lynn Johnson: 2, 6–7, 9, 12, 17, 18, 24, 29, 31, 34, 42, 46, 49, 50–51, 52, 56–57, 59, 60, 61, 64, 66–67, 69, 71, 72, 76, 80–81, 83, 85, 86, 89, 90, 92, 93, 96, 98–99, 102, 106, 111, 113, 116–117, 118, 122, 125.

Photograph of Annie Cogburn on page 38 by Melissa Springer.

It is the policy of
William Morrow and Company, Inc.,
and its imprints and affiliates, recognizing the
importance of preserving
what has been written, to print
the books we publish
on acid-free paper, and we exert our best
efforts to that end.

Library of Congress Cataloging-in-Publication Data
Laskas, Jeanne Marie, 1958–
We remember : women born at the turn
of the century tell the stories
of their lives in words and pictures /
Jeanne Marie Laskas ;
photographs by Lynn Johnson
p.   cm.
ISBN 0-688-15863-3
1. Women—United States—Biography.
2. Biography—20th century.
I. Johnson, Lynn. II. Title.
CT3260.L37 1999
920.72'0973—dc21
[b] 98-21777
CIP

Printed in the United States of America
First Edition
1 2 3 4 5 6 7 8 9 10
BOOK DESIGN BY YOLANDA CUOMO
Associate Designer, Kristi Norgaard
www.williammorrow.com

contents

acknowledgments

My interest in the elderly was ignited many years ago on an unrelated project, when I met an old lady balloonist named Constance Wolf. Over ice cream and champagne she told me stories about her life up in the clouds. She wore her white hair as if it were the crown of a noble empress and taught me that wrinkles were the badge of a life worth living. I first thank Constance Wolf, who died before this project was born, for inspiring me to explore the dignity of old women.

My thanks to Ellen Levine, *Good Housekeeping*'s editor in chief, for coming up with the concept and format and enthusiasm for this project. And to Diane Salvatore, executive editor, for her tireless commitment to the work.

Peter Levy searched throughout the United States and found most of the women featured in this book while performing many other miracles of research. My profound thanks to him. I am also grateful to my editors at William Morrow, Betty Kelly and Doris Cooper.

I'd like to thank Alex, my husband, for loving this project as much as I did, and for feeding all our animals while I was finishing it.

Finally, I'd like to thank the twenty-five remarkable women featured here, and their families, for allowing me to come into their lives with a tape recorder and a notebook. For many, these meetings were physically and emotionally demanding, yet all endured the process with grace and good-will. Their generosity of spirit gives this book life. I pass their stories on with abiding affection.

—Jeanne Marie Laskas

I would like to thank the women in this book for sharing with me not only their precious time but also the wisdom they have acquired over a century. Another generous spirit, my colleague Pamela Willis, helped to make these photographs possible. And my thanks, too, to Maya Kaimal, photo editor, for her tireless efforts.

— Lynn Johnson

foreword

Ellen Levine

Editor in Chief, *Good Housekeeping*

As I write this, we stand on the brink of the twenty-first century. The advances we'll see in the coming century are too vast to even imagine, but the glimmers are electrifying, from cloning to genetic transplants to a "cure" for aging.

One way to get a sense of what's ahead is to consider what's just behind us. At the start of the twentieth century the world did not yet know the lightbulb, anesthesia, the telephone, the car, the airplane. By its close, we'd been introduced to rocket ships, laser surgery, electric cars, the microchip.

But the story of the twentieth century is about more than just machines and medicines—more, even, than its wars and social revolutions. The twentieth century is the story of people—in particular, the story of women.

Over the past one hundred years, women's lives have changed profoundly, more so than at any other time in history. Women stepped into the twentieth century as second-class, sometimes third-class, citizens, mostly denied an education, mostly confined to the home front, mostly restricted from the workplace, from politics, and from the broader life of the world. Of course, women still managed to lead rich and honorable lives, as the stories you're about to read illustrate. But compared with the way we live now, these were lives short on options.

As women step into the twenty-first century, a kaleido-scope of choices awaits us. We can raise a family and/or work, or we can do one and then the other. We can run for office, run a corporation, run a marathon . . . or *all* of the above. Sometimes the choices are difficult, even painful. But at least they are ours to make.

The twenty-five women in this book have lived through one hundred years of change. The colossal shifts of the times were not just newspaper headlines to them; the events arrived literally on their doorsteps. Bessie Marshall found herself inheriting the farm her father, as a freed slave, bought after the Civil War—and it was her help that was critical in allowing the family to secure ownership. And Lois Addy remembers the arrival of the hand-held iron—no more pressing clothes with a heavy slab of steel warmed in the family fireplace! You'll meet a 101-year-old practicing doctor, a tennis ace, a military woman. You'll meet women who struggled—to break the glass ceiling in corporate America, to break racial barriers on Broadway, to break habits and expectations of their own about how far and how fast women could go in the world.

And yet many of the themes in their lives are timeless. There are stirring love stories among these remembrances, romances that survived terrifying epidemics or fearsome world wars. And there are classic stories of mothers making sacrifices for the safety and well-being of their children.

We invite you to hear their voices, marvel at their courage, benefit from their wisdom. The story of the twenty-first century is ours to write. Let us begin . . . in tribute to those who came before us.

introduction

First Lady Hillary Rodham Clinton

The women you'll meet in this book were born at the beginning of a new century. Their stories are the stories of the twentieth century. The people they've known—from Will Rogers and Judy Garland, to W. C. Fields, Shirley Temple, F. Scott Fitzgerald, Franklin Roosevelt, Barbara Stanwyck, and George Gershwin—are people most of us have read about only in books and newspapers or seen in movies. The places they've lived and the places they've traveled remind us just how much the world has changed since they were born.

When Minnie Littlebear, Ethel Coffman, and Bess Hoffman were babies, Utah had just become the forty-fifth state in the Union and gold had just been discovered in the Yukon. Emma Washa, who has written a weekly column for the Boscobel, Wisconsin, *Dial* for thirty years, reflects on one of the most dramatic changes she witnessed in the country during her lifetime: While each of her nine children had a farm, only one of her fifty-five grandchildren does.

These women have lived through the administrations of nineteen presidents, going back to Grover Cleveland. When Thilda and Lena Vangstad were babies, President William McKinley was assassinated and his vice president, Theodore Roosevelt, became, at age forty-six, the youngest president ever.

When Rose Kotz was a baby, baseball was also in its infancy and Boston's Americans vanquished the Pittsburgh Nationals five games to three in the very first World Series. Most of this group was also alive when Orville and Wilbur Wright suc-

cessfully flew the first power-driven airplane in 1903 and when Neil Armstrong stepped onto the surface of the Moon in 1969. Peggygene Evans, who danced in Lon Chaney's *The Phantom of the Opera* and in *The Jazz Singer,* remembers the first talking movie. Annie Cogburn, a registered nurse, remembers the first time she talked on a telephone. Lina Beacon remembers outhouses, washing clothes in pots of boiling water stirred with a poker, the invention of the bra, running water, lightbulbs, and the first trash pickup service.

Lois Addy, who baby-sat for Senator Strom Thurmond when he was a tyke—he's now ninety-seven—says the electric iron is the best invention since sliced bread—although she says sliced bread is a pretty good invention, too. In 1919, she bought her first car for $632. Bessie Marshall bought her first car in 1927 and remembers when electricity came to her home in the forties. Before that, the neighbors would all gather in her yard to listen to her battery-powered radio. When Leila Denmark, who's now the oldest practicing physician in the country, became a doctor, sterilization and anesthesia techniques were primitive. It was her research on whooping cough that led to the development of a vaccine in the 1930s.

Every one of these women remembers the Great Depression and the New Deal. Retired seamstress Rose Kotz says Franklin Roosevelt changed her life. Before he was president, she made $1 a week. New labor laws boosted her pay to $19 a week. Lois Addy, though, will never forgive Roosevelt for ending prohibition.

Every woman profiled here has witnessed two world wars. Frieda May Hardin enlisted in the navy shortly after it started taking women in 1918. She is the only living female World War I veteran. Lina Beacon's husband, Jerry, fought in World War I. Her son's ship was torpedoed by a German submarine during World War II. She remembers the pride she took in helping the war effort by planting a victory garden. Margot Por and her husband, Eugene, spent four years in concentration camps in Europe during World War II. Tomie Ito was among the one hundred twenty thousand innocent Japanese Americans sent to internment camps during the war. Still, she became an American citizen in 1953 and says she loves the United States.

Others endured discrimination as well. Minnie Littlebear was born in a wigwam in Nebraska. When she was fourteen years old, she became one of the generation of Indian children sent to boarding schools to make them "less Indian" and assimilate them into mainstream American culture. Bessie Marshall and Martha Jane Faulkner were both born to fathers who had been slaves. On the other hand, Etta Moten Barnett became one of the first black women to perform at the White House when Franklin Roosevelt asked her to sing "My Forgotten Man" for his birthday.

There is no doubt that one of the most striking developments over the lifetime of this group is the transformation of the role and status of women in American society. Not one of these women could even vote before August 26, 1920. Lois Addy was twenty-seven when she voted for the first time and she's voted in every election since.

These stories remind us that women have always worked, and worked hard, both at home and in the workplace. Most were expected to care for husbands and families even while earning an income. They blazed paths for us, and we stand on their shoulders even now as we struggle to balance work and family in our own lives. But although they had jobs—most as clerks, secretaries, teachers, or nurses—they were never fully partners with men in the workplace or at home. For most of them, the glass ceiling was more like a concrete ceiling and promotion was never a consideration. Many, like Peggygene Evans, who ran a successful chain of dance schools, gave up their dreams and ambitions of a career when they married.

Anita Currey spent thirty-eight years at Guarantee Mutual Life Company in Omaha, Nebraska. With no marriage prospects, a college degree, and even some graduate-school work, she assumed that one day she would move out of the clerical ranks and into a management position. But it never happened. Although she headed the women's division of the Omaha Chamber of Commerce and was appointed by the mayor to the city's library board, Anita never became a manager. Now, with tremendous enthusiasm, she watches the gains women have made in workplaces across America. "You know," she says, "I read in the paper about people being designated as officers. And it's women, women, women! They're vice presidents and presidents. And it's wonderful! I love it! And," she adds, "who knows, there might soon be a woman president of the United States."

Anita's right. There will be a woman president of the United States. Some of us may not live to see it, but it's because of women like Anita and all the other women whose lives we celebrate in this book that it will happen. Every woman who enters a field long open only to men, every woman who casts a vote or runs for public office, who plays sports or shoots for the stars, owes these twenty-five a debt of gratitude. As the beginning of the twentieth century held untold promise for them, the beginning of the twenty-first century holds even more promise for the women of today, their daughters and granddaughters.

As we embark on our celebration of the new century and the new millennium, the president and I have asked all Americans to "honor the past and imagine the future." I want to thank *Good Housekeeping* and its editor, Ellen Levine, author Jeanne Marie Laskas, and photographer Lynn Johnson, but most especially the twenty-five wonderful subjects of this book, who remind us how much Americans have to be proud of and grateful for. We are given the chance to honor their past by hearing their stories and they've helped us to imagine the untold opportunities that await women in the future. They've given us all a very special gift.

WE REMEMBER

lois addy

Reflecting
on a
Time
Before
Autos,
Sliced
Bread—
and the
Vote

Born 1892

Lois Addy, 104, has lived her whole life in Saluda, South Carolina. When she was nine, her father, a judge, moved the family onto the property where her stately brick house now sits, shaded by enormous magnolias. Only the magnolias weren't here then. Neither was the lawn.

"Oh, no, you didn't have grass," she says. "You didn't know what a lawn mower was. The yard was just dirt, the cleanest dirt. You'd scrape it with a brush broom. You'd make the brush broom with branches from the dogwood."

Lois's memories of those days are vivid. She remembers all the trouble it was to keep food from spoiling— for years her mother would hang the evening's supper in a bucket in the backyard well, where it was cool. Later, her father built a cold cellar. Years later still came ice boxes; a man in a horse-drawn wagon would drop off the block of ice every week.

She remembers, too, all the times she had to baby-sit for little Strom Thurmond (who, at ninety-seven, is the longest-sitting U.S. senator in history) when his daddy would visit. Lois's brother-in-law was the senior Thurmond's law partner.

"Strom was just a little fella," recalls Lois. "And we had a gentle horse, Maude, and that boy was crazy about horses. So all I had to do was take him out in the yard and let him ride old Maude."

With her father's many successful campaigns for reelection to the bench, politics was a constant in Lois's life. She wasn't much for it, though. She didn't like the meanness that came over Saluda every election day. Her girlfriend's daddy would be running against her daddy, and all the other daddies would be arguing about who they were voting for.

Of course, the mommies had nothing to do with any of this; women weren't allowed to vote. It wasn't until Lois turned twenty-seven that Congress approved the 19th Amendment, which gave women the right to vote. Lois cast her first vote in the next presidential election (Warren G. Harding versus James M. Cox) and hasn't missed one since.

"You were proud to have a part in the government," she says.

"You had no right to complain about the country if you didn't exercise your right to vote." She won't tell you who she voted for, though—not in the last election or any other. In the tradition of her day, such things are private matters.

Unless, of course, you're talking about Roosevelt. Lois still hasn't forgiven Roosevelt, and she is very public on this matter. "I had no respect for him," she says. "I can't say I hated him because I don't believe in hating anybody. But I had absolutely no respect for him. I didn't have any respect for Eleanor, either."

It was during Roosevelt's administration that prohibition ended. Lois, a lifelong member of the Women's Christian Temperance Union, believes that a good deal of the world's problems can be attributed to alcohol.

"My parents were total abstainers," she says. "I was taught as a child that it sneaks up on you. And I never tasted a single drop of alcohol or tobacco in my life."

In all, there were eleven children in Lois's family, although Lois never knew five of them. "The three oldest ones lived," says Lois, "and then the next five died. They were anywhere from nine months to three years old when they died. You know, like whooping cough or pneumonia. Back in those days, everybody died with pneumonia in the winter, or in the summer they died of typhoid fever."

Lois was the ninth child. She was a happy-go-lucky tomboy who loved the outdoors and hated ironing—at least the way it was done back then. "You had to put the fireplace on, no matter how hot it was, and spend the whole day using heavy smoothing irons kept hot in the fire." Lois thinks the electric iron is the best invention since sliced bread.

"Actually, sliced bread was a great invention, too," she says. "I mean to think, bread you didn't have to cut!"

The automobile was a good addition to life, too (Lois

ONCE A CAREFREE TOMBOY, LOIS ADDY, RELAXING IN HER BACKYARD TODAY (p. 2), donned a frock at age fourteen to address the Women's Christian Temperance Union (p. 3). In 1911, she tilled her college garden (p. 5); a retired art teacher, she does some sketching using her bed as a desk (p. 7).

bought her first car in 1919 for $632), but, really, what Lois appreciated most were paved roads. She remembers the mud. Always having a dirty hem, all the bumps you couldn't see. "And you'd be riding in the buggy and all of a sudden a wheel would go down," she recalls. "And you'd fall into the foot of the buggy. So to have a smooth road, that just changed everything."

Lois also recalls how greatly enhanced life was by the telephone, which came along when she was a young woman. She remembers all the times her father would have some important people visiting his office from out of town and he would invite them home to supper. He had no way of communicating this to his wife. And in those days, you couldn't just throw a dinner together.

"We'd have to run out and catch a chicken and tie up the feet and cut off the head and pluck it and fry it up," she says. "It would take two hours before you could have dinner.

"And to think now," she says, "now you can buy a chicken already plucked. I think that's wonderful."

When Lois was fifteen she met her Prince Charming at a Sunday-school convention. She cites this as the most significant moment in her life. "He was handsome," she says. "He had pretty brown eyes and wavy brown hair." Lois and Marvin dated for two years and became engaged. "But with the understanding that I would get a college education before I got married," she says. It was something she had always wanted to do. And her father was wealthy enough to afford the $140 annual tuition at nearby Winthrop College. "I took the railroad to college," she says. "And then the streetcar. Not an electric streetcar. It was pulled by mules."

And Marvin, a farmer, waited for her. "We got married right after my college," she recalls. "We were completely in love. Mildred was our first child. And then came Katherine two years later. I stayed home all that winter of 1918 because there were measles and whooping cough throughout the land. The baby took whooping cough. And then Mildred took the flu the very same hour Marvin took it."

Katherine died of whooping cough and pneumonia. Six months later, Marvin died, too.

"And I had all the time in the world to grieve," Lois says, looking down at the pretty red cardinal embroidered on the pillow beside her.

Lois tried to support herself and Mildred by selling insurance to farmers. But then the boll weevil blight swept through the South and wiped out the cotton fields. Farmers went broke. It would be decades before pesticides were developed to combat the boll weevil; the cotton industry would not return to parts of the South until the 1950s.

Lois returned home to the house in Saluda where she'd grown up. Her mother was already widowed; Lois's father had died of pneumonia. So Lois supported her mother and her daughter by getting a job as a schoolteacher. "I never went to college with the idea that I would have to make a living," she says. "But now I had to."

She took to teaching immediately, and in no time became a school principal. Her mother took care of little Mildred, and Lois was the breadwinner. "We did fine," says Lois. "We never had a reason to complain."

Five years after moving home to her mother, Lois got a letter. "And it was typewritten," she recalls. It was from Sam Addy, the local banker, widowed, with two children. "He wrote to me about how lonesome he was since his wife had died and would I please correspond with him," she says. "But please, he said, if I chose not to answer his letter, please don't tell a living soul that he had written to me.

"Well, I didn't even read that letter a second time. I pitched it in the fire. I wouldn't correspond with Sam Addy or any other man. Because I could never love anyone but Marvin."

Lois did feel sort of bad for Sam, though. Perhaps she could fix him up with a friend of hers. She told her mother about her scheme. "And my mother said, 'I don't know of a finer man anywhere in this world than Sam Addy.' She said, 'You answer that letter.'" Lois did, but only with a mind to introduce him to her friends.

"And eventually," says Lois, "I found out what a wonderful fellow that Sam Addy really was." She was thirty-one when she married him. "And we had a beautiful, happy marriage." She left her teaching job, and later opened an art school for children in her home. She retired at eighty-one, and was cared for by Mildred, her daughter. Mildred died three days before Lois's hundreth birthday, at seventy-six. Now Lois has eight grandchildren, nineteen great-grandchildren, and ten great-great-grandchildren to look after her.

"And I have had as happy a life as anyone can have," she says. "Of course I have had sadness in it. But I never thought the Lord was picking on me.

"When we were little our father told us to fill our minds with beautiful thoughts. He said to make it so your mind has no room for ugliness. He taught us to keep busy, not just for the sake of being busy, but to be helpful to someone else. Be busy with uplifting things, beautiful things, feel-good things."

PEGGYGENE EVANS

The Dance of Life ❧ Born 1894

Peggygene Evans is not stingy when it comes to handing out her Secret of Youth. "Would you like a copy?" she asks, rising from her chair in the Newport Beach, California, apartment where, at 104, she lives alone. "I'll go get you one," she says, adding, "Ugh, look at me, I walk like a goose."

She's been having trouble walking ever since she broke her hip a year ago and had to quit dancing. She began dancing professionally at age ten.

"Here it is," she says, shuffling back into the room, holding a piece of pink paper. "Oh, now look at me. I'm walking like a penguin."

"Peggygene's Secret of Youth," as the paper says, is: one quart baby oil, two ounces white beeswax, four ounces parawax, a half ounce Borax, and one cup boiled water. "The only danger," she says, "is you have to put the Borax in the very last thing after you finish heating it

in the water. Not boiling it. Just heating it. If you don't, you stand a chance of having everything blow up, so be sure you get to a place where you can, you know, duck."

Peggygene has been putting this mixture, her grandmother's recipe, on her face every night for nearly a hundred years. "And that's the secret of having no wrinkles," she says. "Or at least less wrinkles."

Indeed, her beautiful skin is her most striking feature.

"I don't know that it's called beautiful, but . . ."

Peggygene is a tiny woman, just four feet eleven, and there is an innocence to her manner. It's the same quality that allowed her to double for child stars in the movies when she was well into her forties. She was forty-four when she did the dancing for Shirley Temple, who was ten, in *The Little Princess*.

"No one ever knew how old I was," she says. "We never told."

She was born Peggy Gene Eaton in Louisville, Kentucky, the only daughter of a "big lecturer or something of the sort." She never got to know her parents. They traveled a lot, and sometimes left Peggygene at a Louisville convent to be cared for. When she was four years old, her parents never returned from a trip. They were killed in a train wreck in Mexico.

One of the nuns noticed that Peggygene, who loved to dance around playfully in the convent, seemed to have a gift for dance. "And she called my aunt and told her this," says Peggygene. "And my aunt came and she took charge of me. She loved the stage, and she was determined to get me on it." Her aunt and uncle were childless, and very wealthy. They gave Peggygene a happy childhood. The three traveled together in her uncle's Pierce Arrow, one of the earliest luxury cars, and took her to the best dance teachers in New York City and Chicago. Next stop, Hollywood.

When she was ten, Peggygene was dancing in classical and vaudeville acts, joining W. C. Fields and Will Rogers onstage. "It was hard work in those days," she says. "They picked you up and they kept you up all night long sometimes," she says. The year was 1904— the same year the National Child Labor Committee was organized, largely by women, to promote the rights, dignity, and well-being of children.

In 1925 Peggygene appeared as a prima ballerina in a dance scene in Lon Chaney's classic *The Phantom of the Opera*. In 1927 she danced in *The Jazz Singer*. She was already thirty-three years old when that first talkie came out. And her aunt Ida was still her manager. "She made friends easily and she protected me very, very much," says Peggygene. "After she got through making a deal with a producer, she would say, 'Now, are there any strings attached?' Because it's quite well known that a lot of the stars back then had no talent, they got ahead in other ways." She gives a smirk.

"The couch," she says finally. "That was the thing. The directors and producers would try it with everyone. But with me they couldn't because Aunt Ida would stop them."

It was the casting couch mentality that soured Peggygene's ambitions for the silver screen.

She decided to open a dance school instead. It would be a way for her to protect her future; she was not married and had no prospects. She had never even had time for dates. She was not even sure where babies came from.

"Some people won't believe that," she says. "Because now they know everything at a young age. But my aunt told me, 'You grew in a little nest next to your mother's heart,' and that's what I believed."

And so this sheltered woman, who looked like a child and could dance like a dream, next turned into a savvy businesswoman at a time when few women had businesses of their own. The Peggy Gene School of the Dance opened in 1927. "Trust art, not chance," was its motto. "For they move easiest who have learned to dance."

By the 1940s there were ten Peggy Gene dance studios (she spelled her name differently back then) in and around Los Angeles. Her clients were movie stars, Judy Garland, Loretta Young, and many others. She became famous for her schools. New York City society pages would report on Peggygene's activities whenever she came to town, marveling at all the motion-picture stars who attended parties in her honor, and all the "picture magnates and prominent theatrical people" who would call on Peggygene at her luxurious suite in the Hotel Astor.

And always her aunt Ida was with her. They were best friends. The day of her aunt's death in 1938 was perhaps the saddest of Peggygene's life.

Nearly two decades later, when Peggygene was turning fifty, her life took a dramatic turn.

She was living comfortably in a house in southern California with a housekeeper, a nice large yard, and three wired-hair terriers, including Cuddles, her favorite. A neighbor invited her over for lunch and there was a nice business-

A DEEP LOVE OF DANCE HAS ENRICHED PEGGYGENE EVANS'S WHOLE LIFE (p. 9). She twirled across many a vaudeville and Hollywood stage, even doubling for Shirley Temple, before opening a string of glamorous dance studios that drew such stars as Judy Garland and Loretta Young. In her twenties, she made a bewitching ballerina (opposite).

man there, Hal Evans, who was a friend of the family and a widower with a young son. By the time lunch was over, he asked Peggygene, "I wonder if I could come visiting?"

"And three days later," recalls Peggygene, "he was trying to give me a ring to marry him."

She refused at first, even though she was drawn to him. Did he capture her heart?

"He captured my respect," she says. "He was the first man of my dating season who was honorable and high principled." They got married in 1944. Cuddles and the other dogs were part of the package— but not the rest of Peggygene's life. He would forbid her to dance.

"He didn't like it," Peggygene says. "Wives were supposed to be in the kitchen," she says. "That was a big thing back then.

"I had to sell the studios. I wasn't happy about it at all. But I don't think it hurt me. I loved him. I wasn't in love deeply, but I loved him."

Peggygene raised his son, and discovered that she had a talent for painting, an activity her husband would allow. She painted a picture of herself dancing. She would go on to paint dozens of landscapes and portraits which, ever the businesswoman, she sold. And she got to watch three wonderful grandchildren get straight A's.

Peggygene was eighty years old when her husband died. She felt the loneliness deeply. She picked herself up and traveled the world. "New Zealand, Australia, all over the European nations. I took tours. I'd find a couple that was fairly interested in me, and I'd hang on."

She came home, and began dancing again. She signed up

for tap classes. She joined a group of elderly people who wanted to get a tap act together called The Happy Hoofers. She helped them with their act. "At first they'd hang their hands against their sides and watch their feet," she says. "So by the time I got through with them, they were smiling, looking up, and using their arms!"

Peggygene was back. She danced at charity events and retirement homes with The Happy Hoofers until she was 102. She was busier than ever. She managed an apartment complex. She logged thousands of hours of volunteer work at the nearby hospital. "It just gave me such a good feeling," she says. "Plus, I made really good friends with the eye doctor and the dermatologist, so now they never charge me anything when I go in."

Peggygene's life is quieter now that she can't get around. She spends her days reading history and biographies and classics. She thinks she might be good at writing and just may try her hand at a novel soon.

"And, nobody will ever believe it, but I read the Bible every day," she says. "I'm not a religious person. I don't like the churches. But I'm very spiritual. And some things in the Bible give me a feeling of being protected. I do think there's something, I don't know what, that is taking care of us."

What does she think it will be like in heaven? Will she be a dancer? A teacher? A painter? A novelist?

She thinks on this for a moment. "I think I'd like to do volunteer work," she says. "Well, I don't know if they'll need anybody."

BESSIE
MARSHALL

❧

A Slave's Daughter: Separate—Then Equal

———————

Born 1896

"The Yankees came through here and freed my father," says Bessie Marshall, sitting in a wheelchair in her darkened bedroom. "The colored folks wanted to be turned loose, so they got the Yankees to come through and help." Bessie lives on the Alabama farm that her father, a former slave, bought in 1900. "A white man sold my father this place," she says. "He would sell his land to nobody but colored folks. He was nice. Some white people helped the colored people. Some didn't."

Bessie is 100 years old. Her eyesight is gone now, and she chills easily, so she keeps the heat up high in her small, white-frame house. She wears a wool cap. Memories flow freely from her, most of them scenes from childhood.

"Cotton," she says. "We raised cotton. And corn and sweet peas and peaches. We had plenty of food. We raised whatever we wanted to eat."

A black landowner was something of an anomaly in the post–Civil War Deep South. Most former slaves worked as sharecroppers: The white landowner allowed them to work the land with his equipment and live there rent-free. In exchange for his labor, the sharecropper was supposed to receive a share of the crop's profits, which would go toward buying the land. But, in reality, many white landowners kept black workers so deeply in debt that it would take generations for them to pay the debt off.

But Bessie's father had another source of income. Having served in the Civil War, he received a war pension. It took him four years, but he was eventually able to pay the $100 for the twenty acres of land. And in exchange for plowing the white man's fields three days a week, he got the use of a mule.

As a little girl Bessie worked a full morning on the family farm, and then went to work on white people's farms. "My momma would carry us to their place to chop cotton," she recalls. With a hoe, she and her mother and brother would thin out those cotton seedlings, row by row, field after field. "My momma would get one dollar a day," she recalls, "and me and my brother would get fifty cents a day."

She remembers how fancy the white people's houses were; she liked to sit outside and imagine how pretty the rooms inside might be. "But if you was colored, you couldn't go inside," she says. "If the weather was bad, you had to go in where they keep the cows."

Still, as a child, Bessie knew her family was lucky. Most sharecropper kids lived in shacks on the white people's property. But Bessie's family had their own home, with two bedrooms. The family slept in one room; Bessie's brother and mother slept in one bed, and Bessie shared a bed with her father. "I slept at the foot of the bed," she recalls. "Because my father, he said I kicked."

The other room at Bessie's house was reserved for the preacher who would come to the village twice a month for Sunday services. "None of the colored folks had a company room except us," she says. "So we could take the preacher. And in that room for the preacher my momma had a pitcher in a bowl and a big old kettle you could put on the fireplace and use to heat the water. So he could bathe himself off with it."

Although illiterate, Bessie's parents knew how to work the system and get on the good side of the people in power. During prohibition, her mother won favors from the all-white police—she made wine for them. "She had a stove in the kitchen and she would put a nice tablecloth on the table," recalls Bessie. "And they'd come in there and drink and have a big time. Then they would put a quarter or a dime in a glass jar for her, and tell her they'd come back another day for some more."

Even so, as Bessie grew up, she could see that her parents were easy targets for white carpetbaggers and other opportunists who found ways to legally steal land from the few black landowners. Naive blacks would put an *X* on the dotted line of documents handed to them, effectively giving away their land. Bessie, who finished the seventh grade, could read and write, and so she was able to protect her parents. And she had a guardian angel of sorts: a woman at the courthouse, a white woman, who made it her personal goal to look after Bessie and her family for years to come. "She said, 'Don't you sign nothing unless you get me to see it,'" Bessie recalls. "'They can't make you sign. Bring them up here to me; I'll fix them,' she'd say.

"Well, see, she was nice. And that's how it was. Some white people helped the colored people. Some didn't."

As a young woman in her twenties, Bessie married a local man who decided to move up north to seek his fortune.

"White people come down here from Indiana and got colored folks," she recalls. "They carried you up there and learned you how to make paper. My husband worked in the paper mill while I cleaned trolley cars. You had to pay the white people back for carrying you up there, though. It took a long time." Disillusioned, Bessie's husband decided to move to Philadelphia to try his hand at carpentry and Bessie followed.

She had a son, Wiley, whom she sent back to Alabama for her parents to care for so that he might have a more stable upbringing. But as Wiley reached school age, her parents needed help. "My mother and father got old with nobody to see about them," she says, "and people was taking their money." Thieves would convince little Wiley to bring them money that his grandparents had hidden in the house.

Bessie knew she had to go home and care for her parents and son. By this time she had two other children in tow. "But my husband, he refused to come back here," she says. "I said I would build him a house, but he said no. But you know, like so many of them, he would drink and he would run around."

So Bessie went back to the farm, raised her children as a single mom, picking cotton and milking cows. "We lived good," she says. "We had peach trees and pear trees and pomegranate and pecan trees, and other treats for the children to eat."

BESSIE MARSHALL, SITTING BENEATH A PICTURE OF HER ALABAMA sharecropper parents (pp. 12 and 17): As a child, she helped her family work the cotton fields for 50 cents a day. She took a somber photo, whether captured as a young teenager (p. 13) or a wife and mother living in Philadelphia in 1917 (p. 14) before returning to the South.

Bessie never married again, although she had three more children. She was well known for her talents as a midwife, "catching babies" for anyone who needed the service. And in 1927 she did the unthinkable: She bought a car. And she got a driver's license.

"The white people told me, they said I shouldn't bring my daddy to the hospital in the wagon no more, it took so long. So I got a Chevrolet stick shift. And I would drive anybody who needed it around, if I was going that way. I didn't mind if they was white or colored, anybody I could help, I liked to help."

Electricity didn't come to rural Alabama until the 1940s, but Bessie remembers having the first battery-operated radio around. They'd hang it outside in the oak tree, and neighbors would come from all over on Saturday nights to hear the fights. Shortly after that, electricity came, and Bessie got a television set.

"Oh, I put it up and my yard would be so full of people looking at that thing talking," she says. "Some of the white people would come; they ain't never seen something like that. And the colored people, too. They would say, 'Make it talk!'"

When asked how the world has improved in the last century, Bessie stops and thinks a while. She sits hunched over in her wheelchair, a portrait of Martin Luther King Jr. and John F. Kennedy overhead.

"Ain't nothing better about today that I can see," she says finally.

"Oh, Mom," says Frances Taylor, sixty-one, Bessie's only surviving child, who cares for her on the farm. "Aren't some things better now?"

But Bessie is blank.

"Like now you got a bathroom in the house; before you had to go outside," prompts her daughter.

"Yeah, that's better," Bessie allows. "But I say most things was better before. It wasn't like it is now, everybody for theirself.

"Before, people would help each other, colored or white."

Brooke Astor

Sharing the Wealth ❧ Born 1902

"I can't believe how much I do, either," says
Brooke Astor, ninety-five, who has been called
"the First Lady of New York City." "I'm on the go
all day long, every day. Isn't that ridiculous? And I
walk and I swim, and I'm a wreck, as you see."

Hardly. Sitting in her Park Avenue office in
Manhattan, Brooke Astor is, as usual, dressed to
the nines. Today she has on a navy polka-dot dress,
a string of pearls, a stylish blue hat with a wide
brim, and white gloves. She's just returned from
Harlem, where she attended the dedication of a
statue honoring the late Duke Ellington. The rest
of her day is meetings, meetings, meetings. And
her dog is sick; she is waiting for a call from the
vet. And what about her good friend Prince
Charles? She's hoping he received her fax this

morning and that he's feeling better. She saw him
on television last night and he did not look well.

Brooke Astor is loved around the world for her
good works. For the past four decades she has
devoted her life to giving money away.

"No, I had no background in this at all," she
says. "When Vincent died, I just said 'Look, I
want to run it.'" Vincent Astor, her third husband,
controlled the Vincent Astor Foundation, whose
$57 million in assets were to be used "for the alle-
viation of human misery."

Vincent himself had done little with the foundation. When he died in 1959, it was Brooke who
gave it life. "I said, 'I want to return the money,'"
she says. "Because old John Jacob Astor, that was
Vincent's grandfather, he made his money in New

York real estate. And I just thought that was the best thing to do, to return the money to New York."

And so in the last forty years she has channeled more than $175 million not only to giant institutions like the New York Public Library, the New York Zoological Society, and the Metropolitan Museum of Art, but also to tiny organizations that receive far less attention: people renovating decrepit urban housing, people saving all-but-forgotten landmark buildings, people who work with the illiterate, the homeless, the destitute, the key word being "people." Unique among philanthropists, Mrs. Astor made sure to know and visit everyone to whom she was giving money. "And I think that aspect of it has really made my life for the past forty years," she says.

The phone rings. It's the vet. "Hello? What? Well, at three o'clock in the morning she woke me up with an awful yelp. She doesn't want to walk. She doesn't play. Do you think she's got cancer again? You don't. Well, she's not well. Yes, I'll bring her down. Thank you. Me? I'm feeling so-so. I'm tired. I've been away."

Brooke Astor is a working woman fully in charge of her own life, right down to pet care. She thinks the end of this century is certainly the best time in history for women. "Women now have so many resources," she says. "When I was coming along we had only one: we flirted."

Not that flirting didn't have its good points. For one thing, it was fun. It's that sense of play, as well as style, that she sees slipping away from American society. "It's changed socially," she says. "In the old days there were such parties. You dressed up and you had music. Scott Fitzgerald and all those people, they were so much fun. We had games. They had words or a slogan you had to think of. Charades. And I remember acting out all sorts of funny things. But nobody does that anymore. It was a simpler time.

"I think now people are watching television instead. People are rushing home to watch *Charlie Rose* or something. And they don't read as much. That's gone. They don't have long love affairs now, either. It's just sort of, 'Your place or mine?' I think long love affairs are wonderful fun."

Her first, at the tender age of sixteen, started out as fun

but turned to disaster. Young Brooke was the only daughter of a career marine officer and a fun-loving mother. The trio lived all over the world—Annapolis, Panama, Peking—before settling in Washington, D.C. When she was sixteen she got an invitation to attend Princeton's senior prom, and jumped at the chance. She met Dryden Kuser, the handsomest young man at the dance. "And I told him I was a neorealist," she recalls. "I didn't know then and I don't know now what it means. Almost a realist, I guess. But he said he was a neorealist, too. And so I thought this was fate."

After the dance Dryden pursued Brooke with flowers and letters, and Brooke was in love. But there were a few strange things about Dryden. "He'd never been to school," she says. "He'd been brought up by a private tutor. And then he was finally sent to college with twenty-five thousand dollars to spend, which was like a million today. And then he was given a private chauffeur. Yeah. Ridiculous. I should have known. Mother should have known. And father was away."

At seventeen, she married Dryden. He turned out to be a drunk, a womanizer, and a batterer. "I could take anything," she says. "I'd had a wonderful childhood so I had a lot to be happy on. So I got through it. I grew up. And then when he wanted a divorce, I was thrilled. Because I knew I could have my child all to myself."

Brooke was twenty-four with a baby, Tony. "I wasn't sour," she says. "I'd had a miserable eight years but still I wasn't sour at all. Or going around saying how terrible everybody was. I didn't."

Two years later she met Charles Marshall, a New York stockbroker. "I absolutely adored him," she says. "Marshall was the love of my life." They married, and for

---

A GREGARIOUS GRANDE DAME WHOSE TIRELESS PHILANTHROPY HAS EARNED her the title of First Lady of New York City, Brooke Astor has always adored animals as well as people. Today she caresses her dachshunds in an exquisitely furnished room (p. 18), but even at age seven, she was never far from a pet (p. 21). Holding on to her uncle (*left*) and father (*right*), one-year-old Brooke took her first steps in Washington, D.C. (p. 22).

twenty years Brooke was a happy wife, entertaining guests, traveling, making friends, and just being with Marshall. "In the evening, we'd sit by the fire and read aloud to each other," she says. "The same book. And then we'd discuss the book afterward. I mean, things like that," she says with a gleam in her eye.

On Thanksgiving Day, 1952, Marshall died in her arms of a heart attack. It was the lowest point in her life, the point that allows her to conclude that no, she would not say she has had a happy life. "But you don't have a life, really," she says, "unless you had bad times."

Only a few months after Marshall's death, Vincent Astor began courting Brooke. He was sixty years old and ranked among the richest men in America. To outsiders, he did not seem to be Brooke's type. He was moody, brooding, unsociable. But Brooke fell in love with him and they married. He wanted her all to himself, and Brooke devoted her life to him. After his death six years later, she devoted her life to the foundation with which she would make her mark. She is now putting the foundation to rest, and getting on with the other important business of life: writing poetry.

"So you see I couldn't have married again," she says. "I wouldn't have had the time. And now? Well, now it's pretty late for me. But we'll see."

margot por

From the Misery of the Holocaust, a Miracle

———————

Born 1906

Margot Por, ninety-two, rarely talks about the four years she spent during World War II in Nazi concentration camps. Her husband, Eugene, remarkably spry at 103, has even more trouble with the subject; at family gatherings he will quietly leave the room if the topic is brought up. The memories are simply too painful. And yet imbedded in those memories is the couple's cherished love story.

Margot was born in Munich, the daughter of a successful cutlery manufacturer. "We had a very comfortable, huge apartment, well, not as comfortable as here," she says, sitting in the living room of her elegant apartment in a high-rise on Philadelphia's Main Line. As usual, she is dressed up in a pretty print dress; Eugene is likewise, in his finest crisp white shirt buttoned to the top.

She was a happy child, gifted musically, and unafraid of the world. She and her older brother attended a neighborhood school, where they were taught to be patriotic Germans. "I had Jewish friends and non-Jewish friends. You didn't give it any thought back then," she says. Upon graduation from high school, Margot was sent to the prestigious Berlin Academy of Music to study piano. Her career as a concert pianist was sidetracked, however, by her mother's plans for her to marry Walter Herz. Walter's mother was also a party to the scheme.

Two babies later, Margot and Walter were living in a small apartment in Munich in January 1933 when Adolf Hitler's Nazi party took power. Hitler's aim was to build a new Germany, the Third Reich. And he believed that this country could achieve greatness only when the "inferior people" were no more. Margot couldn't quite understand any of this, but somehow, as a Jew, she was among this targeted group.

"So we moved from Munich, away to Holland," says Margot. "We did not think Hitler would ever make it to Holland. We were a bit more stupid than some other people who ran farther out."

Some thirty thousand German Jews fled to Holland (among them, Anne Frank and her family). Others sought refuge in France, England, and America. Margot's brother went to Portugal.

Margot and her family made a home in the suburbs of Amsterdam. Walter started a business with a neighbor, and the children attended Dutch schools. For nearly seven years they felt insulated from the troubles in Germany. In many ways Holland seemed like one of the safest places in the world for Jews. The country had, after all, been neutral during World War I, and when Germany invaded Poland in 1939 and World War II began, Hitler said he would honor Dutch neutrality.

But he didn't. In 1940 German troops invaded Holland. The Jews there were sitting ducks. With Germany on one side and a heavily guarded North Sea on the other, there was no escape. No forests to hide in, as in France and Russia. Nowhere to go. More than 70 percent of the Jews in Holland would perish in the Holocaust, the highest death rate in any country occupied by the Germans except for Poland.

As Anne Frank would write in her diary, German soldiers walked the Dutch streets and, apartment by apartment, rounded up the Jews and arrested them.

"We were taken to Westerbork," recalls Margot. Westerbork, in northeast Holland, was a "transit camp." Most people didn't stay there more than two weeks. On Monday nights the names would be read. On Tuesday mornings the train would arrive. Over a thousand prisoners a week would be put in cattle cars and sent to "labor camps." At least that's what Margot and the rest were told.

It was January 1942 when Margot and her family arrived at Westerbork. Erica, her daughter, was thirteen and Ernest, her son, was nine. "It was a big camp," Margot recalls. "Walter had to go to the men's barracks. My daughter was sent to the girls' barracks. And I got a little room with my son."

Their names were not on the list of those going on the train. Instead, they were picked to work at the camp because they had citizenship papers provided by an aunt in Palestine (now Israel), giving them the official right to emi-

"I THINK IT HELPED US SURVIVE," MARGOT POR SAYS OF FALLING IN LOVE with her husband, Eugene (p. 24), while both were imprisoned in Holland in 1942. Before the war's horrors, she enjoyed a day of cycling with her children by her first marriage (p. 27). After the war, Margot and Eugene moved to the United States and settled on Long Island (p. 29).

grate. Prisoners with such papers from other countries were put in a separate category by the Germans.

Margot and her family would stay two full years at Westerbork. Margot was put in charge of the women's barracks. "I had to keep a book with the names, and be sure the beds were made in the morning," she recalls. "And people were always coming in and others going out. Every week the same thing. The names would be read. The train would come. And we didn't know for sure what happened to them. But we had a feeling no good was happening to them."

Her eyes well up. She looks at Eugene. He seems to take the cue. He seems to know it is time for him to say something.

"We didn't know anything about Auschwitz," he says, referring to the gas chambers where most of the prisoners from Westerbork were actually destined.

Margot and Eugene met at Westerbork. He was brought in to be her assistant as a barracks leader. Margot had never met a gentleman quite as kind as Eugene before. Eugene, whose wife was put to work elsewhere in the camp, had never met a woman with quite so much charm as Margot. They fell in love. She does not believe her husband knew about her affection for another man, so occupied was he with administrative duties assigned to him by German soldiers. Her daughter, Erica, was worried for her mother. "Watch out," she'd say. "That man is after you."

"She didn't like the situation at all," says Margot. "But I think it helped us survive. There was something else besides misery." Plus, as prisoners, it was doubtful that they would survive the war. "And so we thought, 'Take it while it is.'"

Their relationship continued until the day Eugene and his wife were put in cattle cars and sent away. Margot had no idea where he was going, but it was clear that she would probably never see her love again. Shortly afterward, in February 1944, German soldiers ordered Margot and her family, including her parents, who had since joined them in Westerbork, onto a train. "You are leaving now," they said. The family was not told where they were going.

They were sent to Bergen-Belsen, a starvation camp in Germany, the same one where Anne Frank would die.

"Bergen-Belsen was barracks, just barracks," Margot recalls. "And people died daily. Hourly. Malnutrition, sickness, hardly any water. . . . It was a very difficult time there. Lice, everybody had lice. That's how we all got typhoid fever. And once a day they would bring in large metal containers. Soup, a kind of soup. Turnip soup. We had only turnips." Her father couldn't take it anymore. He died of a heart attack.

In April 1945, German soldiers again gave orders. "You are leaving now," they said. This time, Margot and the Bergen-Belsen prisoners were put on a forced march of some seven miles to reach a cattle train destined for Auschwitz. Some twelve hundred prisoners were on that fourteen-day train ride, eating raw potatoes and anything else they could find. Walter had typhoid fever, and Erica was also sick, but Margot's mother was even worse off. Margot managed to find her mother a place to lie down on the floor of the train. Her mother died in her arms. They buried her alongside the tracks while the train was stopped one night.

On the fourteenth day the train stopped again. Only this time there were two Russian soldiers on horses outside. They could speak no German, and the Germans could speak no Russian, but the point nonetheless was put across: The war was over. They were free.

"We were weak," Margot says. "We took some cart and put Walter in it." He was battling typhoid fever. "And Ernest and Erica and I pulled that thing to the next village." They found housing in a nearby village where Russian soldiers ordered the German villagers to take them in. "And then Erica got so sick she was delirious and wanted to jump out the window. Ernest and I had to hold on to her. And then I was able to go in the basement of that house and I found there preserved cherries, which I brought up. And that was the first elegant food we had had in years."

Walter and Erica survived and the family returned to Holland by July 1945, where friends took them in. "And the very first evening the doorbell rang and we came down the stairs looking.

"And it was him," she says, motioning toward Eugene. She beams like a teenager. "He had an armful of red roses."

He had been sent to Buchenwald, a forced labor camp in Germany, and had survived, although his wife had not. He had come looking for Margot. He found her, thanks to a document provided by the Red Cross, which published lists of survivors and where they were housed.

"And I said, 'Mr. Por, how are you?'" Margot recalls, and it is at this point that she has trouble speaking. She shakes her head. She dabs her eyes. She still can't believe the miracle.

Margot and Walter divorced. Margot received word from her brother, who had spent the war years in America and was living as a farmer in Vineland, New Jersey. Eugene left a few days before Margot; his brother had invited him

to Manhattan. When Margot and the children arrived at Ellis Island, there was Eugene, waiting for her.

"And in America?" she says. "Well, everything was great, everything was fantastic, from stockings up. We didn't have decent stockings at all, so really, from stockings up, everything was outstanding, wonderful, great. And eating too much ice cream, oh, it was just, to start life again!"

Two years after their arrival here, Margot and Eugene were married at a New York City courthouse, and went out for a boiled-beef dinner. Eugene got a job with the same firm he had worked for in Europe before the war, an international paper company, and the family settled on Long Island. Since the day they became American citizens, neither Margot nor Eugene has missed voting in a single election, not even the tiniest local race.

"And we've kept together now for fifty or more years," she says. "And we are very fortunate to be together, to like each other, to love each other, and to manage together so

well." Finding true love, she says, could be the secret to Eugene's longevity. "I cannot give myself credit," she says. "But I think sticking together was good for both of us." She smiles at Eugene. And he smiles at her. There is relaxation in the air. She made it. She did it. She told her story.

Her daughter, Erica, now seventy and living in an apartment upstairs, has been listening to her mother today. Erica is able to speak openly about spending her teenage years in the concentration camps, but knows how difficult this is for her mother and stepfather.

"You did great," she is saying. "Just great." She is proud of Eugene for staying in the room. He has done it for a reason. He is 103 years old and he has something he needs to say. He motions toward Erica, holds her arm, and speaks into her ear.

"We are thankful to America," he says, quietly taking a breath. "Please make sure this comes across. We are proud to be Americans."

anita
currey

The Glass Ceiling,

Circa 1930

Born 1902

For the thirty-eight years she
worked for the Guarantee Mutual Life
Company in Omaha, starting in 1929,
Anita Currey imagined herself in
a management position. She had a lot to
offer: a college degree and graduate-school
work; a fiercely competitive spirit
that enabled her to defend a state tennis
title for more than five years; and
leadership qualities that kept her at the
helm of the women's division of the
Omaha Chamber of Commerce. Even the
mayor of Omaha would recognize Anita
Currey's skills when, in 1947, he
appointed her to the city library board.

But corporate America was another place
entirely.

"You couldn't crack those guys," says
Anita, now ninety-six, sitting in the small

apartment she keeps at a personal care center in Omaha.

"I mean, one day, one of the officers of the company came to me and said, 'Anita, you're going to be the first woman officer of this company!' There must have been some talk. But later he told me that two of the other officers, they said women were good for scrubbing the floors or something.

"Finally you just forget it. I just ignored it. Because in my own mind I sat pretty high."

In all her years working for the company, Anita was never promoted to a management position.

Anita Currey was born in Louisville, Kentucky, one of five children. Her father worked for a construction company. "But somehow or other he wasn't able to make money," she recalls. Her mother handled the business side of the family, investing money she received from her parents. "So we profited from that," Anita says. "Not lavishly, but okay."

The family relocated to Omaha in 1918, with the promise of more construction work. Anita returned to Kentucky for college.

"Oh, yes, I am a graduate of Centre College!" she says. "You never heard of Centre College in Danville, Kentucky?

"They beat Harvard. Six to nothing. 1921." It was an away game, a football championship. Anita can still remember all the townspeople standing outside the telegram office. "They had the street blocked off. And you would wait for the telegram to come down. 'Centre made five yards!' Every play. And we'd shout, 'Wooo!'"

She was a freshman and, at five feet eleven, a gifted athlete. She would go on to be the undefeated tennis champion of her college. It was the most terrific time of her life. And to top it off, she was in love.

His name was Bill. They met in choir practice. She caught his eye. When she excused herself to go to the ladies' room, he also excused himself and waited for her outside the door. And when she came out, he said, "Hello." He escorted her back to choir practice. "And that was the entrance into our romantic life," she says.

They dated, 1920s style. "In our college, boys could make dates for a Saturday night," she recalls. "They had to call before one o'clock in the afternoon. And then maybe a dozen or more boys would stand by this door to the dorm that was going to be opened at seven-thirty by the night watchman. And here were all the gals on the other side of the door."

The couples had to stay in the house. "But there were several rooms," she says. "You could find a spot. And there were ferns. And Bill and I would sit down so we were hidden by the ferns. So then Bill could reach over and steal a kiss.

"And then at nine o'clock the bell would ring. And they'd have to leave."

Bill and Anita got engaged. But he didn't want to get married until he could earn a living. So after college he returned to his home in New York City and Anita went back to Nebraska, where she was already becoming known for her athleticism.

In 1920 she was the formidable "newcomer from Kentucky" who would go up against "the charming and very efficient" Mary Gant in the 1920 Nebraska state tennis tournament, the first for women.

"Attractive Maids Enter Tennis Tourney," headlines read. And there was a picture of Anita in her tennis gear: an ankle-length skirt topped by a loose-fitting blouse. Anita beat Mary in two straight sets with scores of 8–6 and 6–1. Anita would win the championship again the next year, and the next, and the next. Then, in 1924, there was that bad call.

"Yeah, Clara Miller messed me up," she recalls. "She hit it out and it was ruled in. But I never argued with the referee. No, for goodness' sakes, no. You'd die of a broken heart before you'd argue with a referee."

Nowadays, she points out, such arguments are commonplace in the world of sports.

"But I guess now these people have piles of money," she says. "If you have fifty thousand hanging on you at a tennis match, you're going to fuss."

Did she make any money from her sport?

"Never! It was the 1920s and tennis was a beautiful game. No money or favors at all. You just played.

"And let me tell you, the game of tennis has changed so much. This little teenage kid now that is a champion—that's not right. That mother is just pushing that kid. I disagree with what she's doing."

Anita stopped playing tennis to go to work.

"You bet," she says. "In the fall of 1929, this terrible financial problem was coming." Construction came to a halt, and so her father was completely out of work. And now there were nine people in the house, including several of Anita's brothers, who had also been in construction, and their spouses and children.

Anita supported the family by getting a desk job at the Guarantee Mutual Life Company for $90 a month. "That was a heck of a lot of money," she says. "I put the food on the table."

She continued to write to Bill. "But you could tell it was fading," she says. "Back then, you didn't just hop a train and move to New York." At least not without a husband waiting at the other end. And Bill still was not ready to marry.

Anita worked in the policy provisions and correspondence department, and performed her duties with pride. She was an organizer; during World War II, she rallied her fellow employees to help in the war effort. It was her idea to start a surgical dressing unit where employees could volunteer their time to fold bandages for the Red Cross. Sixty-three employees, all women, contributed their time. They got their picture in the company newsletter, and a thank-you from the officers of the company, all men, to the "fair sex employees."

She had never set out to be a career woman. "But when I saw that I wasn't going to get married," she says, "boy, I wanted to be president of the company. Or I wanted to be in the upper bracket. I wanted to be an officer.

"Yes, I did believe I would get that chance. I truly did."

When she looks at corporate America today, she becomes animated. "Look at women!" she says, sitting up in her chair. "You know, I read in the paper about people being designated as officers. And it's women, women, women! They're vice presidents and presidents. And it's wonderful! I love it! I mean, all the industries. And my word, there are so many. And I have a young friend who comes out here and visits me for lunch once in a while. And she's in her late forties. And boy, don't you know she's an officer of the company? Just rolling in here on a long lunch hour. That's what they're doing! And I love to see it.

"And who knows, there might soon be a woman president of the United States. I think that's a possibility. I certainly do."

Anita has an optimism about the future that is infectious. No longer able to be a player on the court, she is a spirited cheerleader on the sidelines.

And as for the past, well, she has just begun cleaning it up. She has, she acknowledges, never forgotten Bill. "He was a good boy, a good boy," she says. He married someone else, and died of cancer in the 1960s. And all this time Anita kept the mementos of their time together, the letters, the dance cards, the photos.

"And a couple of nights ago, I finally threw them away," she says. "I finally did it. Because he was no longer in my life." She looks down at her hand, and twirls the ring on her finger, the ring Bill gave her.

Anita retired from the Guarantee Mutual Life Company in 1967. She received a letter of thanks from management, acknowledging her contribution to the progress of the company, "and especially to the men in the field."

A STAR COLLEGE TENNIS PLAYER, ANITA CURREY PROUDLY DISPLAYS ONE OF HER trophies in 1927 (p. 30). Seventy years later, she reflects on a long career in the insurance business (p. 31). In 1925 Anita and the five other female seniors at Kentucky's Centre College often gathered under this tree between classes (p. 32). When the Depression hit, she supported her parents and siblings—"I put food on the table."

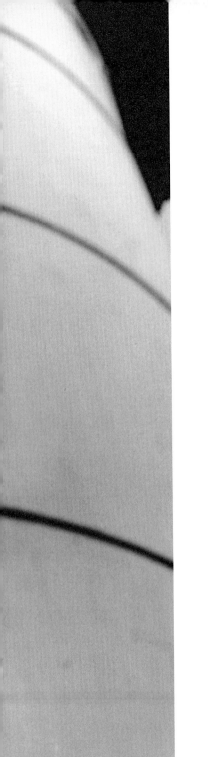

connie small

A Lighthouse Keeper's Wife ❧ Born 1898

For twenty-eight years Connie Small, ninety-seven, lived as a lighthouse keeper's
wife on the rocky coast of New England. It was a life of extraordinary isolation—and
adventure. She would sometimes go four months without seeing a human being
other than her husband.

"I remember one day feeling so sad," she says, sitting in the small room
she occupies today in the Mark Wentworth Home in Portsmouth, New Hampshire.
"It was Easter. And I had on my wedding suit, and the most beautiful blouse,
embroidered with flowers. And a hat that had peacock feathers." Newly married,
she was living in her first lighthouse, Avery Rock, three miles from the mainland
midway up the coast of Maine, and her husband had gone to shore—
a forty-five-minute rowboat ride away—for groceries and household supplies.

"And here I was sitting on a rock pile in the middle of nowhere," she says. "I was so
alone. And I remember I looked down, and there was a little puddle between the rocks,

with a little sea urchin in there." She picked up the urchin.

"I can see the water today, going through my fingers," she says, cupping her hands. "And I looked at that little animal and I thought, 'Why should I feel sorry for myself when I've got the world right in my hand?'" A world to explore and investigate.

"That," she says, "was a turning point."

She was born Constance Scovill in Lubec, Maine, the easternmost point of the United States. One of five children, she grew up next to the sea. Her grandfathers had been sea captains, her uncle was a lighthouse keeper, and two other uncles had been lost at sea together. Her father worked for the U.S. Life Saving Service, a precursor of the U.S. Coast Guard.

"You could see the ships crash on the rock and the vessel would be destroyed," she recalls. "And I can remember my father at the cannon, and the beautiful brass powder can." The cannon would shoot a special lifesaving buoy out to the vessel. Men could climb aboard the buoy and float to shore. "He saved many, many sailors," she says.

When Connie turned thirteen, she developed debilitating asthma. "I would be in bed with it, very, very ill, for many weeks at a time, and so I couldn't go to school because I couldn't keep up. Back then they didn't know about allergies." Years later she would learn that her condition was actually an allergic reaction to the family's Chihuahua.

Her sheltered and lonely life improved considerably when, at seventeen, she met Elson Leroy Small, a tall, blond Merchant Marine serving in World War I, who was home on a brief leave. It was love at first sight. "Just as soon as we walked into each other's life," she says, "we knew we wanted to stay there."

When the war ended about a year later, he came back for her and she accepted his marriage proposal. Then he said, "But do you love me enough to go live in a lighthouse?" He had been offered the caretaking job from the U.S. Lighthouse Service (which, in 1939, was incorporated into the U.S. Coast Guard).

"Well, I had to stop a minute with that one. But I looked at him, and I had to say yes."

They moved into the Avery Rock lighthouse in 1922. Connie was twenty-one and Elson was twenty-five. "We had no telephone, no electricity, no refrigeration," she says. "We couldn't keep fresh food. Elson would buy fresh meat, and we'd put it in the sink in the water. We could keep it for a couple of days. I learned to can. I canned everything. I was so frightened of running out of food."

It was a test of survival for the young couple. Connie remembers a blizzard that came suddenly one night. "I had to run," she says. "I had to shut all the shutters, three inches thick, so the waves wouldn't come through the glass and bury us right in the sea. And Elson was violently ill. And I had no knowledge of sickness, but I took his temperature and it was a hundred and three. He became delirious and I couldn't do a thing with him until he spent his energy and collapsed in bed. He was in a coma for three days. And here I was all alone. And not able to tell anybody we were in trouble. And I had to keep the light burning."

It was the lighthouse keeper's mission, his duty to the world. And her duty, as his wife. Lighthouses (which are now automated, no longer requiring live-in personnel) have been used to safeguard mariners since early times. Constructed at important points on a coastline, the lights guide ships sailing on coastal waters. An extinguished light could spell disaster. Maintenance of the light was a complicated task requiring exacting attention to a system of weights and pulleys that kept the sophisticated crystal lens turning and flashing at precise intervals. As a lighthouse keeper's wife, Connie learned how to work the equipment. She was not on the payroll. She would never receive a pension.

She believed that her husband was dead, during that blizzard at Avery Rock. Her task now was to figure out how to preserve the body. She remembered her mother saying that

CONNIE SMALL HAS NEVER LIVED FAR FROM THE CRASHING WAVES OF THE rugged New England coastline (p. 34). In 1921 she and her cousin scaled the thirty-foot ladder of Maine's Lubec Channel Light at high tide (p. 37). Of the first lighthouse she tended with her husband, Elson, Connie says, "We had no telephone, no electricity, no refrigeration."

you used alcohol to do this. She got the alcohol. "And I stood outside his door for twenty minutes trying to get up the courage to go inside," she says. When she finally did, she heard something, a faint voice: "I'm hungry."

"That was my miracle," she says humbly.

Connie and her husband lived at Avery Rock for four years before moving on to other lighthouses along the New England coast. It wasn't until she and Elson moved to St. Croix River Light Station on a small island on the St. Croix River, near the United States/Canada border, that she found paradise. There were sandy beaches, and tourists who visited for picnics. No longer was she isolated and frightened and hungry. She had a garden, chickens for fresh eggs, and a cow providing milk.

"It was a playground," she says.

World War II interrupted their heaven on earth, however. Elson was called to serve. Another lighthouse keeper was brought in to work the lighthouse, which meant that Connie would have to leave her paradise. She was forty. She was forced to a move into a hotel, then a boardinghouse, and then was taken in by a friend of her mother's for the duration of the war.

When her husband was released from the service, the two went back to the St. Croix River Light Station. Soon, they moved to their last lighthouse, Portsmouth Harbor Light in New Castle, New Hampshire.

Elson retired as a lighthouse keeper in 1947 after the U.S. Coast Guard assumed responsibility for that lighthouse. The couple moved to a modern house in Eliot, Maine.

Elson died of cancer in 1960, when Connie was fifty-nine. "He's still here," she says. "To me, he's going to open that door someday and walk in." With no pension, Connie had to a make a life for herself. She could hear him encouraging her, as he had so many years before, telling the girl with asthma that she could do anything she set her mind on. She got a job at a department store, then as a resident in a dorm at Farmington State College, in Farmington, Maine, eventually taking on duties as substitute dean of students. When she was eighty-five years old, she published a book, *The Lighthouse Keeper's Wife* (University of Maine Press, 1986), and began lecturing about her days on the edge of the sea. At ninety-seven, she is still at it.

"So far I've delivered 521 lectures," she says.

Sometimes she tells people about the time she and her husband were introduced to their first electric lighthouse, the one in New Castle, New Hampshire, in the 1940s. It was quite a modern invention compared to the old kerosene-powered ones that required a full twenty minutes to light.

"And now it was just a button!" she recalls. "And I was so excited to push that button." And so she did.

"And . . . I didn't feel anything," she says. This was strange. The light had come on, as predicted. But where was the thrill? She had expected her first experience with electricity to be more exciting than this.

"I wondered about that for a long time," she says. "And then I realized that before we had to put twenty minutes of ourselves into lighting that light. But now, to just push a button? It didn't mean anything. We hadn't given anything.

"You have to give of yourself to have anything important."

annie cogburn

Nursing, 1920s Style

Born 1893

At 104, Annie Cogburn lives alone. She does her own cooking, laundry, grocery shopping, and gardening, and she dresses up pretty each Sunday to walk to the eleven A.M. service at the West Asheville Baptist Church. How does she make it across busy Haywood Road, with cars whizzing this way and that?

"Well, now, I look both ways," she says. "Wouldn't you?"

Annie is five feet eight inches tall, slender, and delicately featured. She really doesn't think of herself as old.

"Now, where would I find the time to sit around and think about myself?" she asks. "I'm too busy. Always have been."

Annie still lives in the handsome brick house her late husband built for her more than seventy years ago. A registered nurse, she retired at eighty, when she switched to volunteering. She attributes her longevity to "a good body," which was the result of fresh corn bread, buttermilk, and "plenty of pig meat."

She grew up Annie Reel, the third of fourteen children on a farm near Marion, North Carolina. All the children worked in the fields hoeing corn, pulling fodder, digging potatoes, milking cows. The entire family would gather each night for dinner around the long kitchen table and discuss the next day's chores.

"We worked and we went to school and we just didn't know too much about the world," she says. "We didn't know about meanness or anything. We were taught to be good and not tell stories, and that's just the way it was. It stuck with you."

At sixteen she started working at the local textile mill, which was a lot better than farming because at least you were out of the hot sun. She remembers a measles outbreak in the mill, and how it was to lose so many of her friends to that dreaded disease. She contracted measles, too, and eventually pneumonia. "And the doctor came to see me."

Such visits were rare. Annie can remember just a few other times when the doctor was summoned to the area. "Everybody knew he was coming. People would be out on the road, flagging him down, asking him what was the matter with them.

"Well, he had himself a box of pills. And he just gave everyone the same pill. And they would get better. Just so they got a pill from the doctor, they were happy."

Little did Annie know that she was getting training for a career in health care, 1920s style. Her nursing career happened almost by accident. She was in her early twenties. All her friends and sisters were getting married, but Annie was too busy for boys. She wanted to see the world. She went to visit a sick friend in Asheville. The doctor came and performed a kitchen-table appendectomy and there was no one around to assist but Annie. The doctor was so impressed by her work that he asked her to assist in another home surgery. He then convinced her to go into nurses' training.

One of her first experiences at Mission Hospital was to assist in an amputation. That was a lot harder than the appendectomy. "When they started sawing that arm off," she recalls, "I went down on the floor with it." This was in the days before sophisticated anesthesia, and the sterilization of surgical instruments was primitive. "We really didn't have sterile things then," she recalls. One of Annie's jobs was to boil the instruments in the small nurses' kitchen, three hours a day for three consecutive days. "And on the third day they were supposed to be germ-free," she says.

Annie still has her nursing school diploma hanging on her living room wall. Earning that degree remains the proudest moment of her life. "Well, if you had been able to get a diploma from a school like that, wouldn't you be happy?" she says.

She was twenty-seven when she graduated, "an old maid" by her family's reckoning. She earned $5 for twenty hours of duty, and lived in an apartment with two other nurses. She remembers the most remarkable invention appearing during those years: the telephone. "They said you could talk in this thing and it would carry your voice. I didn't believe it. Then, the first time I tried it out, there was someone I knew on the other end of the line, my aunt Anna. I recognized her voice. And that was the only way I would ever have believed it."

While still in her late twenties, Annie met William Cogburn, an Asheville police officer thirteen years her senior. He proposed.

"And I said, 'Well, everybody wants to get married. But I don't want to get married without a house.' And you know what? Bill Cogburn went and he built me this house. So then I had to get married."

He designed the house with an oversize living room and dining room, determined to make the Cogburn home the one where church Christmas parties would be held. And they were. Bill and Annie were happy, a two-income family—with a brand-new baby. It was shortly after William Jr. was born that Annie's mother contracted tuberculosis back on the farm. After her mother died, at fifty-seven, Annie brought her younger sister, then sixteen, to live with her. Her sister

---

ANNIE COGBURN LEANS AGAINST HER BELOVED BLUE CHEVROLET (P. 38). SHE decided to become a nurse after assisting a doctor at an emergency kitchen-table appendectomy. With a boyfriend in her nursing-school days (p. 39) and with friends in the Asheville mountains (p. 41; Annie is on the left).

helped raise Annie's son so that Annie could go on working.

"Of course, you had your family on your mind all the time," she says. "But the Lord helps you get accustomed to a lot of things. I worked because we needed money. If we didn't need money, I wouldn't have worked."

The only time Annie took a break from her work was when she nursed her husband during his dying days. It was the saddest time of her life. She was fifty-nine, a widow. She would never forget Bill. She would stay true to him. She would never leave the house he built for her.

Nowadays, Annie's son, age seventy, a widower, lives nearby. He comes by with groceries, and tends to Annie. And he begs her to please stop driving around the neighborhood in her blue Oldsmobile.

"I don't know why," she says. "Anybody who has driven as much as I have and never even hit a fire hydrant—why would they feel like I can't keep on doing it?"

But Annie takes her son's nagging in stride, as she has taken most of life. She is not one to complain, not one to whine about the state of the world.

"The only thing I see," she says about the difference between the world she knew in her youth and the world she knows now, "is that there's so much learning now. People didn't used to have much learning. But they had good common sense. Today it's the other way. A lot of learning, not so much common sense."

Then again, some might say that a 104-year-old woman attempting to walk across busy Haywood Road lacks a certain amount of common sense.

But Annie says an adventure is an adventure. You never know what might happen. For instance, one recent Sunday she had a little excitement. "I got all dressed up in a pretty white-wool coat suit," she recalls. "And don't you know, I hung my heel over the step out there and fell. A man coming down the street, he saw me. He pulled his car up on the churchyard, and he came over. And there's my pretty white coat suit with blood all over it."

She had broken her shoulder. An ambulance rushed her to the hospital.

"And I got to stay at that hospital several days," she says. "I had such a nice time. All those nice people. I told them, I said, 'I'm going to do that again sometime.'"

thilda and lena vangstad

Through the Years, Side by Side   ❧   Born 1901

Except for a seven-year separation early in their careers as college teachers, identical twins Thilda and Lena Vangstad, ninety-seven, have spent virtually every day of their lives together. Try as they may, they cannot think of a single thing they disagree on.

"Well, there must be something," says Thilda.

"Let's see," says Lena.

"Oh, she's the better cook," says Thilda.

"No, she is," says Lena.

They look at each other, think about this.

"Neither of us is a very good cook," says Thilda.

They are identical in every way, from their hairdos to their smiles to their purple outfits to their earrings and brooches. The twins were born in a farmhouse just up the road from their present home overlooking Osakis Lake, near Minneapolis. Their parents had emigrated from Verdal, Norway, to this land of wheat and oats and corn, and had eleven children in all.

"We were seven and eight," says Thilda.

"And we were a unit," says Lena. "It was always, 'The twins did it.'"

They walked two miles a day to a one-room schoolhouse, graduating from high school with the thirteen-member class of 1919. Academically, they were identically smart, often scoring the same grades on tests, often getting the same few answers wrong. As many twins report, they intuitively knew how to "communicate" without words.

"I would be taking the test and I would think, 'Oh, Lena is not going to know the answer to this one,'" says Thilda. "And I would just think very hard and I could send the answer to her."

Sure enough, Lena would later report a struggle with the test question, and note the way in which the answer suddenly hit her.

The phenomenon became second nature to both; years later it would come in handy. One time recently they got the idea to paint their kitchen and agreed on light rose as the color. Lena left the house to go buy the paint. Thilda, at home, began to think rose was all wrong for the kitchen. She thought: pale green. She thought pale green, pale green, pale green as hard as she could. Sure enough, Lena came home with green paint instead of pink.

Careers as teachers came naturally to Thilda and Lena, thanks to their mother, who encouraged further schooling after high school. They graduated from the University of Minnesota, where both also earned master's degrees and soon they settled in Langdon, North Dakota, where both landed teaching jobs. Their lives seemed set. They lived together, shopped together, and still dressed alike. And why not? They liked the same things.

In 1937 Lena accepted a job offer to teach at Valley City State College, and so the twins were separated for the first time.

"But you can even get used to an amputation," Thilda would say at the time.

For seven years the sisters were apart, although they would spend summers together back on the farm in Osakis. Then came the offer to Thilda; she, too, accepted a job teaching at Valley City State College. For the next twenty-six years they were identical twins with nearly identical jobs. "Miss Lena," as she was called, taught education and psychology, while "Miss Thilda" taught social sciences.

They wore their positions with pride. They had succeeded in climbing the ladder of academia, not the simplest task for women of that era.

"But still the men made more money than the women," says Thilda. "The thinking was, Well, a man has a family to support. And we were single. And so when they look at the credentials, they're the same. But they thought the man needed a better job."

"And that was not right," says Lena.

"I don't think so either," says Thilda.

"But I think now women are getting that worked out a lot better," says Lena.

"I hope so," says Thilda.

The two enjoyed their years at the college. They were roommates who devised rituals that they would continue for the rest of their lives. One day Lena cooked, the next day Thilda cooked. Laundry, housework, shopping, and all the other chores were thus divided, without so much as an argument or complaint. And still they dressed identically. They lined up their outfits in the most methodical way, outfit one, outfit two, outfit three.

The twins retired from the college in 1971, and returned to the place of their birth. They are happy here. Still active

and healthy, they take frequent car trips, as far away as Washington, D.C., and Los Angeles. "One drives one day, the other drives the next," says Thilda.

"And when we're home," says Thilda, "if it's my day to cook on Sunday, then she drives to church,"says Lena.

"And she drives home," says Thilda.

"It's childish, you know," allows Lena. "But that's why we get along—we take turns."

"That's what keeps the peace," says Thilda.

"If nations of the world had the same program," says Lena.

"They'd get along," says Thilda.

"But they don't seem to speak the same language," says Lena.

"And we do," says Thilda. "Sometimes when we're in church, I might get the idea that we need something at the store. And I let her know that, just by thinking it."

"And so we'll get in the car," says Lena. "And I'll just start driving to the store, because somehow I know."

"We have a very even life," says Thilda.

"I feel sorry for people who don't have a twin," says Lena.

"It must be very strange," says Thilda.

People in Osakis embrace the Vangstad twins as their own. "But now they stare at us more," says Lena. "Because we're a couple of old ladies coming along, they take another look."

"And they always want to know what the difference is," says Lena.

They think about this one again. Surely there must be something they disagree on, some issue, some political stance, some taste in jewelry or clothing or literature.

"Oh, I know!" says Lena. "She likes Promise margarine."

"Oh, and she likes Fleischmann's," says Thilda.

"But I'll make the sandwiches and I'll use Fleischmann's on hers sometimes," says Lena. "And she doesn't notice."

"Yes I do," says Thilda.

"That was Fleischmann's last night," says Lena.

"Oh," her sister says. "Oh, well."

THEY LOOK ALIKE, THEY SPEAK ALIKE, SOMETIMES THEY EVEN THINK ALIKE—AND ninety-seven-year-old Thilda (*left*) and Lena (*right*) Vangstad wouldn't have it any other way (p. 42). The Minnesota twins at age six. (p. 45).

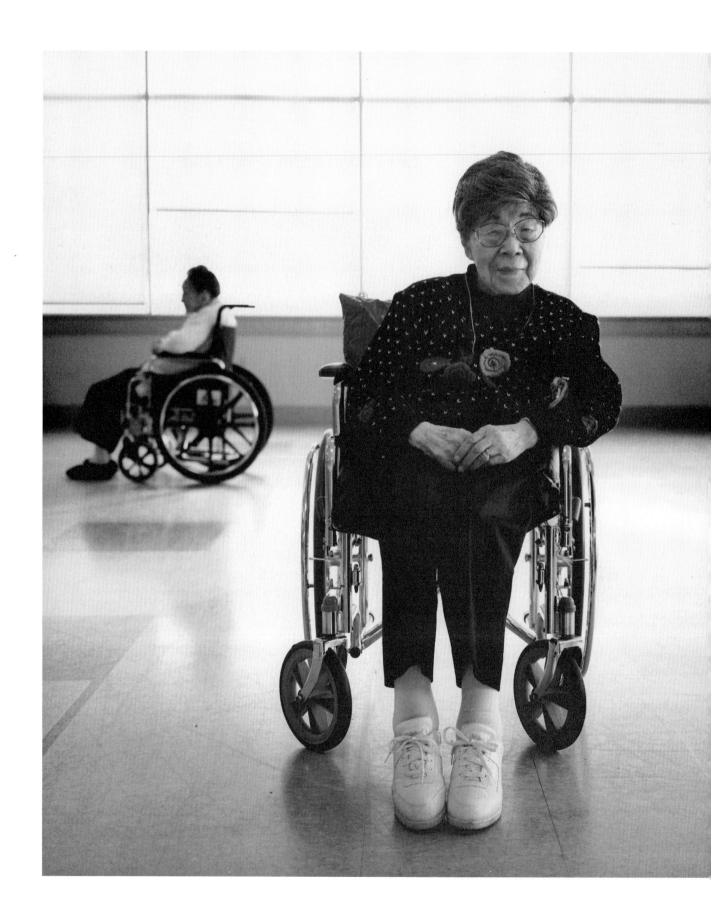

tomie ito

A Prisoner in Her Own Land

Born 1899

Like many Issei, or first-generation Japanese-American immigrants, Tomie Ito, ninety-nine, has a saying about the year and a half she and her family were imprisoned in a World War II internment camp.

"*Shikataga-nai*," she says, shrugging her shoulders here in a Seattle nursing home. "It means, 'That's the way it is; there's nothing I can do,'" says a translator.

"That's not the way I look at it," says her daughter Lily Wallace, seventy-seven, a Nisei, or second-generation Japanese American, who was also interned, and who is decidedly more resentful. "I mean, we are Americans, you know?"

Many scholars consider the internment of Japanese Americans during World War II to be the most serious violation of constitutional rights in United States history.

Tomie was born in Nagano, Japan. Her parents lived in Korea, where her father was a member of Japan's military police, and so Tomie was raised by her grandparents until she was eleven, when she joined her parents at Yokosuka, a military base outside Tokyo. She eventually received two interesting marriage proposals, one from the wealthy son of a liquor-store tycoon and another from a gardener who had his sights on America, the land of opportunity.

"And a lot of people thought I was stupid to want to go to America," she says. "Because people will discriminate against you and not accept you. And they said if I married the rich man I would have a life of prosperity. But I knew how those men were. They have mistresses and geisha parties and play around.

"I chose the man who was tasteful, who didn't drink, didn't smoke, and was very nice to me."

And she chose America. She and her husband, George, settled in the Seattle area, where they lived and worked on a relative's three-acre pig farm. When they finally earned enough money to move to town, Tomie got a job at Grand Union Laundry, while her husband started his own landscaping business. They had three children. They were happy. The land of opportunity had certainly lived up to its reputation.

And yet in that same land there was a distinct anti-Japanese sentiment brewing, especially on the West Coast, where more than twenty-five thousand Japanese immi-

grants, who had left Japan in search of employment, had flooded the U.S. labor market. Then, on December 7, 1941, Japan attacked Pearl Harbor, causing the United States to enter World War II. The attack mobilized people's prejudice against the Japanese. Years of anti-Japanese sentiment erupted into hate and suspicion—and hysteria.

"I remember someone from the government came around and took the knobs off our radios," recalls Lily. "So we couldn't send short-wave messages, or whatever, to Japan with our war plans or something.

"And then they took our knives, all our cutlery. I guess so we couldn't go around stabbing white people," she says with more than a hint of sarcasm.

The hysteria reached fever pitch when, on February 19, 1942, Franklin D. Roosevelt signed Executive Order 9066, which called for the eviction and internment of all Japanese Americans—nearly 120,000 people who were accused of no crime, and two thirds of whom were native-born Americans.

"First we were rounded up and sent to the fairgrounds," recalls Tomie. "We could bring two shopping bags full of our things." They were housed in livestock stalls for about two days. "And from there they put us on a train."

"Don't call it a train," Lily says. "It was a stinking old cattle thing. It stunk like cow manure."

Ten "relocation centers" had been hurriedly built in desolate areas of Arizona, Arkansas, California, Colorado, Idaho, Utah, and Wyoming. Thriving Japanese communities in Seattle, San Francisco, and Los Angeles became ghost towns.

Tomie and her family were sent to Minidoka, a desert area of Idaho populated by coyotes.

"It was very windy," says Tomie.

"And all sagebrush and dust," says her daughter, who was

"You go along with what the government tells you," says Tomie Ito with equanimity of her year and a half in a Seattle internment camp for Japanese citizens during World War II. With her siblings before immigrating to America (p. 47; Tomie is the tallest) and with her daughter, Lillian (*left*), and a friend (p. 49), and with a dear companion (pp. 50–51).

twenty-one when she arrived at the camp.

"My family was put in one room to live," says Tomie. "And I was made to work in the kitchen. My husband, I didn't want them to know he was a gardener, because I feared they would put him to work in the hot sun. So we never told."

Conditions were poor. This was a prison. The barracks were tar-paper shacks, and meals were taken communally in mess halls, with waits so long that violence flared. The camp was surrounded by barbed wire and towers, with armed guards surrounding the perimeter. "People who tried to escape—some of them, they went crazy or something—they tried to run," recalls Lily. "And they were shot."

Tomie prefers to recall the one ray of hope in this otherwise dismal situation: a Catholic priest who helped the prisoners. She knew Father Leopold Tabesai from Seattle, where she and her husband had converted to Catholicism. He was not Japanese. When the internment program began, he came to the camp in Idaho and saw to it that the prisoners were treated fairly.

And when, on December 17, 1944, President Roosevelt announced the revocation of Executive Order 9066, Father Leo made sure that Tomie and her family had a place to go. Prisoners were not allowed to leave unless they had papers showing that they had a job somewhere. This was something of a catch-22. How could you get a job if you weren't allowed to leave? Some prisoners in some camps languished there for months. Many had lost everything while imprisoned—houses, businesses, belongings. And the West Coast was not yet a friendly place to return to. Word got around quickly that, back in Seattle, homes were defaced with graffiti: "Death" and "No Japs Wanted." In a cemetery south of the city, headstones with Japanese names had been toppled.

Father Leo found Tomie and her husband a job in Detroit.

"It was in a hospital," says Tomie. "A very nice hospital. I worked in the kitchen. And my husband worked in there, too."

After a few years, the family returned to Seattle, where Tomie worked as a housekeeper and her husband rebuilt the landscaping business he had lost.

In the 1970s he had a stroke, and moved to a nursing home where Tomie visited daily and read to him. He died in 1978, a full decade before the United States government provided restitution and an apology for the Japanese-American internment fiasco. Some sixty thousand Nisei who had been interned died before that apology.

"I became an American citizen in 1953," Tomie says proudly, as if unaware of the irony that lies beneath that claim. How can she be proud to be a part of the very people who so blatantly violated her rights?

She doesn't see it that way.

"I love the United States," she says. "I think to be a good citizen, you go along with what the government tells you. And maybe in the camps we were more safe. Because in the towns people were throwing rocks at us."

"We are not fighting people," says Lily. "And that annoys me sometimes. I mean, my generation is much more resentful of what happened than my mother's. But we don't talk too much about it, either. We hold it in. We're kind of real meek about the whole thing, you know? But what can we do?"

"*Shikataga-nai*," Tomie says.

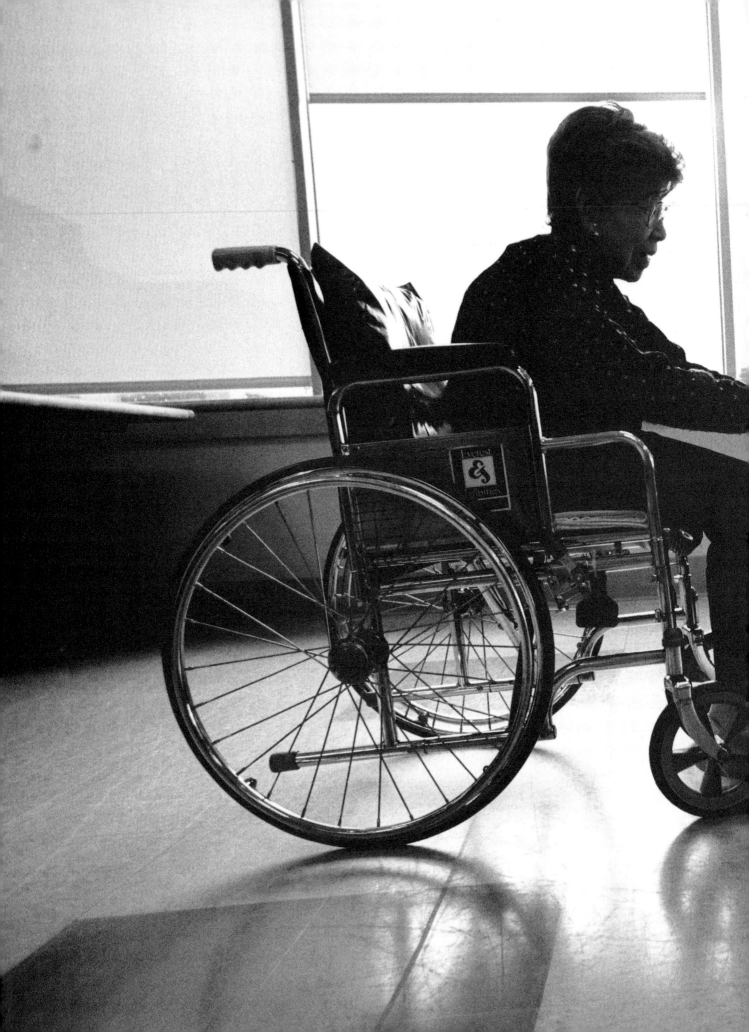

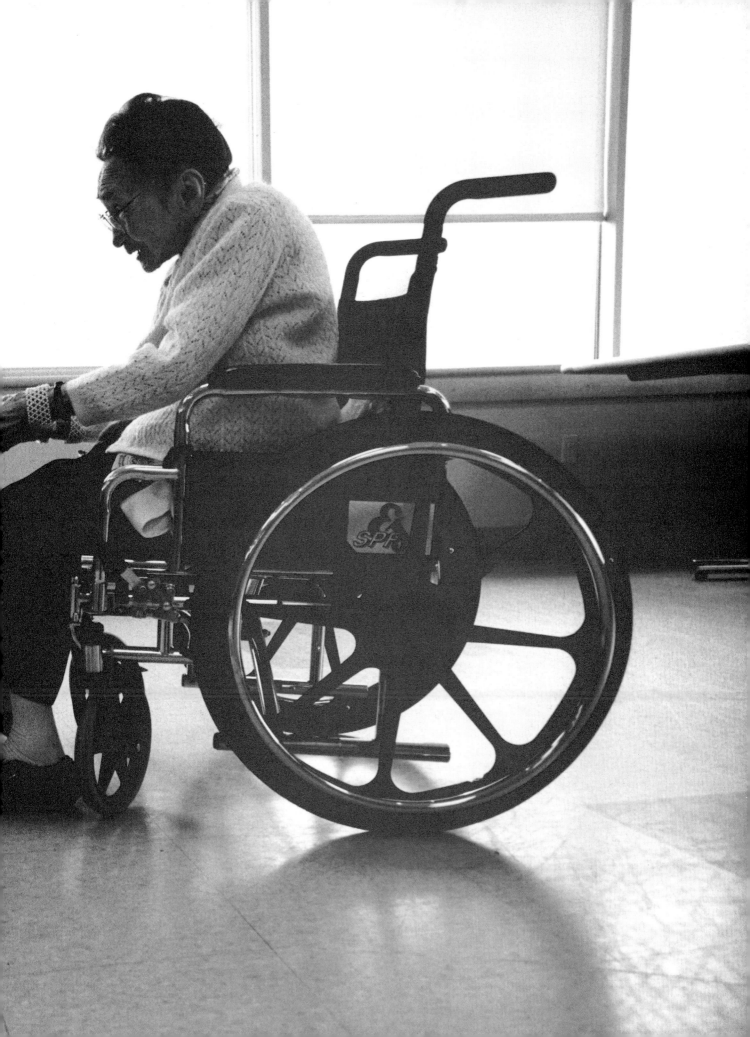

LEILA
DENMARK

The Doctor Is In—
Seventy Years and Counting

Born 1898

"I reckon I've had more patients than any doctor on Earth," says Dr. Leila Denmark, 100, the oldest practicing physician in the country. She still sees anywhere from fifteen to twenty-five patients every day, four days a week, in a pediatrics practice that has been around for seven decades. Her office, a dilapidated farmhouse near Atlanta, Georgia, is just a skinny pathway away—past a couple of bird feeders and just beyond two sprawling magnolias—from her kitchen door.

"Watch your step," she says, climbing an old cinder block that doubles as a stoop to the back door of her office. She's dressed in a smart wool skirt and a pretty white blouse with a bow. "Okay, now you want to plug in that space heater?" she says, entering the examination room. "And I'll get this one over here." It's Saturday, her day off, but she got a call about a sick child, and so Dr. Denmark is here. It is not uncommon for her to rise at two A.M. if necessary, get dressed, and come to the office to see a sick child.

"I know, some doctors will say, 'Don't call me at night,'" she says. "But I think it's an honor that people want me to help them. So I don't mind it at all."

The examination room is sparse, a desk, a window, a poem on the wall. "And my table," she says. "I'm practicing medicine on the same table I had in nineteen twenty-eight," she says, rapping her knuckles on it. Someone once bought her a shiny new table to replace this one. "And I said to take that thing out. I can't check a baby better on a three-hundred-dollar table than I can on this. I said give that money to a baby so she can have some food or some clothes.

"I never have wasted money to show off my office. I'd have to charge more for that, you know."

Dr. Denmark charges $10 for a first visit, $8 for every visit after that. She has no receptionist, no appointment book. People simply show up and write their names on a clipboard, then wait their turn. They are poor people and they are rich people. They are people whose mothers and fathers and in some cases grandparents were once nurtured by the tender hands—and prescriptive words—of Dr. Denmark.

The phone rings.

"Dr. Denmark," she says authoritatively. "What's the problem?"

The man on the phone has called to say his son has the flu. "Okay, I'll call the druggist with some medicine," she says. "What's that? Oh, I see. Uh-huh." The man says his son has been acting out, picking fights with his brother. The father has tried everything to get him to behave. "I see," Leila says. "Okay. Here's what you need to do. Don't lecture him. Don't argue with him. That's right. You're the only audience for that little boy to have. And if it bothers you, he's going to keep it up as long as it bothers you. So don't ever mention how he treats his brother again. Just be nice to him.

"If you were a great actor and you got on the stage and everybody left, you'd quit acting. Right? That's right. Okay. Bye-bye."

Dr. Denmark has never once prescribed a dose of Ritalin, today's drug of choice for children with behavior problems. For that matter, she has never prescribed a dose of cough medicine. "I try to find out what's making them cough instead of shutting them up," she says.

She was born Leila Daughtry, one of twelve children raised on a prosperous farm in the South Georgia town of Portal. Her father was the town's mayor, and she was a happy child who loved to care for the animals. "And I liked flowers," she says. "I remember putting wilted flowers in water and watching them come back again. So early on I got the idea of making things come back."

She attended a two-room schoolhouse where she met the man who would become her husband, John Eustace Denmark. He lived two farms down the road. When she finished school, she figured on becoming a teacher—the only career path she'd ever seen a woman pursue—so she went to Tift College in Forsyth, Georgia. "And a professor fixed me up a place to dissect, and I began to get interested in science and medicine."

By the time she graduated, she was engaged to "Mr. Denmark," as she calls him. But he took a position with the State Department, and was sent to Indonesia—no wives invited. Instead of sitting around and waiting for his return in a few years, she applied to medical school. She was

accepted at the Medical College of Georgia, the only woman in her class. In 1928 she would become the third woman ever to graduate from that medical college.

"And those four years of medical college could never have been more perfect on this earth," she says. "Those were the nicest boys, I tell you. They treated me like a sister. I was just one of the bunch."

On this point she gets worked up. "I have never been discriminated against as a woman," she says. "I never had anybody, any indication of anybody, rejecting me doing the things I have done because I'm a woman.

"I don't know where all this comes from today. I mean, men are wonderful people. I don't understand this. Today there is a fight between women and men. Never was there a war in my day. A man would hitch your horse for you. And he'd help you get in the buggy. And when you got up to the house, he'd open the door for you. Now women think that's an insult.

"It's silly. It sure is. We're not having any fun. And we should have fun. We live in the most wonderful time in all history."

Leila speaks like a preacher with a mission.

"I believe that women should have the right to do anything they want to do," she says. "And I don't want any woman to have a child unless she wants it, but if she brings a baby into this world, that's her responsibility. I don't care if she's president of the United States of America! Her baby comes first.

"Day care has wrecked the nation," she says. "Eighty-five percent of the kids, Monday morning they will go to a day care center, and many will stay there till six at night. And they'll come home to a tired mother and a tired father. Supper to cook, and the house a mess. And there's no peace. No peace.

"You can't raise a child that way! Those little kids are being raised according to the ways of other little kids. They can't follow the parents' way, because the parents didn't rear them. The mother didn't have time to fool with them. She's off doing something 'worthwhile.' That's what they say, doing something 'worthwhile.'"

For her part, Leila is the first to admit that she had it easier than most. She married Mr. Denmark three days after she graduated from medical school. He was on the fast track toward wealth—he eventually became a vice president of the Federal Reserve Bank—and so Leila could afford live-in help. In 1930, when her daughter, Mary, was born, she moved her practice into her breakfast room. She had already accomplished many "worthwhile" things. Her research on whooping cough led to the development of a vaccine for that disease in the 1930s.

"I never had to make a dime on medicine," she says. "Mr. Denmark made the living. So I could give my time to the poor."

Medicine was a ministry for her. She could have retired—at any age. She almost did when she turned eighty-seven. She and her husband had moved from suburban Atlanta out to the beautiful land they owned in Alpharetta. They built a lovely mansion with white columns where they could live out their last years. But Leila had her eye on the old farmhouse in the nearby field—the one where people had once made moonshine. It was falling to pieces. She imagined what it could be like if she got it fixed up a little. She called her grandson. "I said, 'Can you fix it up for me? I'll just have a place where I can see patients occasionally.'"

He scrubbed it, painted it, made it habitable. He hung a hand-painted sign outside, "Office Hours: Monday, Tuesday, Wednesday, Friday, 8 A.M. to 3 P.M."

"And now I'm seeing as many patients here as I did in Atlanta," she says. Her husband died in 1990, at ninety-one. And Leila keeps on. "I've not taken a teacupful of medicine in my life," she says. She credits her longevity to her strict eating habits: three meals a day, each with a protein, spaced five and a half hours apart because "your stomach empties out every five and a half hours." She drinks only

---

THE OLDEST KNOWN PRACTICING DOCTOR IN THE COUNTRY, Dr. Leila Denmark sees patients in a modest office next to her Atlanta home (p. 52). By age twenty (p. 53), she had decided to pursue medicine. She married three days after graduating from medical school and had a daughter, Mary (p. 54). Today Dr. Denmark still sees patients of all ages (pp. 56–57, 59).

water. "No juice, none of that bottled stuff." And she never, ever eats junk. Not even on her one-hundredth birthday.

"I did not have one bite of that cake," she says. "Not one taste."

She has no plans to retire. "Not until my obituary is in the paper," she says. "It would drive me crazy if I had nothing to do," she says. "If I start resting, I'll start judging myself. And then I'll get depressed. You can't get depressed if you're busy.

"Okay, now, does this room feel warm enough?" she asks, going over to tend to the space heater. Her patient is due any minute.

The phone rings again.

"Dr. Denmark," she answers. "What? No, it's okay.

What's your problem?" She listens for a while. "And now the brother has pinworm, too?" she says. "Did you see them? Are you quite sure? Okay, why don't you come by on Monday. That's right. There's no reason to worry about it. It's not going to hurt him. No, you didn't do anything wrong. What? Why are you crying?"

The woman explains that her husband has been scolding her, blaming her for her children's pinworm infestation.

"Oh, my," says Dr. Denmark. "I think that whole household is upset." She looks down at her feet, thinks, and finally comes up with a prescription. "You go gather the family up," she says, "and everybody go on a picnic today. Okay? That's right. Bye-bye."

ethel coffman

A Passion for Fashion ❧ Born 1895

Ethel Coffman worked for forty-six years at Rankin's Dry Goods Co., once the fanciest department store in Orange County, California. She can still remember the outfit she wore on her first day on the job. The year was 1913. "I wore a hat," she says. "And a short-waisted skirt down to the ankles, and shoes that tied up to the ankles, and thick cotton stockings. My blouse was up to the neck. And, of course, I had my gloves." It was the working woman's attire of the day.

Today, at 102, Ethel lives in a sunny room at the Santa Ana Town and Country Manor. She's dressed in a bright pink shirt, a print skirt, and a white shawl. Her white hair is puffy, and piled on top. She has, she says, seen a lot of changes in the clothes women wear.

"Oh, we had such a beautiful glove department," she says, recalling her days at Rankin's. "And, you know, your gloves were fitted back then. Just like your dress, your blouse, your corset, and your brassiere. You never bought something off the rack. Everything was fitted to the individual."

Ethel Coffman was born in Elkhart, Indiana, the daughter of a self-made man with an adventurous spirit. Her mother died when Ethel was just nine. Her father took her and her twin, Esther, and her younger sister, Mary Frances, on the journey of a lifetime.

"He caught the California bug," she says. "We went on a train. And with us was our Little Auntie, bless her heart. We always called her Little Auntie." She was no relation to the family, but joined it to care for the children. "She never married. She gave her life to us."

The family settled in Santa Ana, where Ethel's father took a job directing the choir in the Methodist church Ethel still attends today. "And my sisters and I walked a couple of miles to school every day," she says. "Of course, all the roads were dirt. And I remember when it rained, how much fun it was to plow through that mud!"

A new course of specialized training for girls, commercial studies, was just hitting schools in California when Ethel entered high school. It was an era when women were stepping out of the house and into the workplace, and Ethel's father wanted his daughters to be prepared. "He foresaw that we'd probably have to earn our living," she says. "And so instead of classical studies, we had bookkeeping and spelling and typing and shorthand."

Shortly after high school, Ethel got the job at the department store. It was an exciting place to be. Factory-made clothing had released women from sewing machines and sent them to the stores.

In the 1920s fashions changed dramatically with the postwar feeling of independence. It was the Jazz Age. Gone were corsets, up went hemlines. The look was long and lean. Makeup became the rage—rouge, lipstick, heavy mascara—all to the horror of the older generation.

Ethel moved quickly up the ranks at the department store, from cashier to credit manager, personnel manager, office manager, and, finally, store manager. Her sister Esther also worked at the store, and her younger sister, Mary Frances, was a schoolteacher. None of the women was married, and in 1939 they got an idea.

"Esther said, 'Let's take my two hundred and fifty dollars and build a home.' I had a little savings, I think three hundred dollars maybe. And with that we built our home."

The down payment was able to secure them a $6,500 mortgage, which paid for the lot and a three-bedroom house.

"It was very pretty. We loved it. I guess it was a little bit unusual for women to do that. Most people I knew had husbands."

Ethel had always hoped to get married and raise a family, and she remembers the day she finally surrendered to the fact that true love might never happen in her life. "I looked ahead," she says. "And I didn't see any man in my life. And I decided to be happy with whatever came. I made a very defi-

ETHEL COFFMAN, WHO WORKED FOR RANKIN'S DRY GOODS CO., "a company that had ideals," for forty-six years, mulls family photographs taken at the turn of the century (p. 60). In 1939, with a $300 down payment, she bought a home with her twin sister, Esther, photographed together as toddlers in 1896 (p. 63). Today, Ethel browses through magazines at her California home (p. 64).

nite decision that I was going to find happiness with what-ever was in my life, instead of complaining about what wasn't.

"And of course you can find happiness, if you are able to help somebody. You can usually find somebody that needs help. Even a pat on the back. Or a good word."

One person Ethel and her sisters were able to help was Little Auntie, the woman who raised them. They took her into their home and looked after her until the day she died.

Ethel also became active in her community. She began serving on the board of Goodwill Industries in 1935, and is still on it today. And then there was her loyalty to Rankin's Dry Goods. "It was family owned," she says, "like so many businesses back then. And the family took such good care of us, even during the Depression. Mr. Rankin called all the

employees together and said, 'We're going to weather this. Nobody's going to lose their job. We'll just do the best we can.' So that's what we did."

The Depression did a number on women's fashions, sig-naling the end of the carefree flapper era. Hemlines plum-meted and waists went back up to their natural position. Probably the biggest shopping day in history that Ethel can recall was the day in 1939 that nylon stockings became available.

"Oh, boy!" she says. "They had to stand in line to get to the stocking counter! I mean, that was a big excitement. You could wash them out at night and they'd be dry in the morning. And the first ones were pretty heavy. But later they became sheer, and then they started making them in

different colors. I remember I bought a suit of apple green with stockings to match!"

But nylons got pulled from the market at the beginning of World War II. Patriotic women were urged to turn over their stockings to the scrap drive so they could be converted into yarn for military use. Women's nylons were recycled as ropes, parachutes, and tents.

In many ways the government dictated women's fashions during the war years by issuing a limitations order that aimed to save domestic fabric production. The order banned such items as cuffs and full skirts. Even the height of women's heels was fixed to a maximum of one and a half inches.

Rankin's Dry Goods Co. survived the Depression and the war. It wasn't until 1959, two years before Ethel's retirement, that the store fell on hard times. "And it was purchased by a company that was looking only for money," she says. "And they spoiled the name. They didn't keep up the store. They got everything they wanted out of it. And finally the store went bankrupt, and closed."

Ethel was sixty-eight. She got a job with the county, where she worked until she retired at seventy. She is glad to have lived and worked in a century when businesses were still, as she puts it, "human."

"I'm glad I had my business experience when I did, with a company that had ideals and lived up to them," she says. "Mr. Rankin never cheated anybody, or made false advertising; he was always aboveboard. Well, now, business is kind of dog-eat-dog, you know? They do things that are, shall I say, questionable. I mean, you can't comprehend it. I don't try."

Ethel has lost both her sisters and is now very much alone in life. She does not complain. She has lived at the Town and Country Manor for about three years now, and makes a point of finding what there is to love about it, the birds outside her window, her friends. "And cooking class!" she says. "Twice a week we have cooking. And, you know, probably nobody attending that class will ever cook again. But we get a bite, a taste of whatever the teacher cooks. And so it makes me happy."

Happiness, she says, is something you choose.

sister
regina
heyl

❧

Answering God's Call

Born 1902

At the Pittsburgh monastery where she lives with sixty-nine other Benedictine nuns, Sister Regina Heyl, ninety-five, rises each morning at five-thirty. She dresses in her habit, tucks her gray hair beneath the corners of her veil. She gets in her wheelchair and heads down to the kitchen. She butters the toast, arranges the jellies just so. Before heading to chapel for morning prayer, she helps the crew with the dishes.

These might seem like menial tasks for a woman of her stature, a summa cum laude graduate of the Duquesne University class of 1932. A woman with a master's degree in Latin, a geometry, algebra, physics, and Latin teacher who used to tutor the bishop.

But to Sister Regina, no act for the good of the community is too small.

When asked the secret to a vigorous life in old age, Sister Regina does not respond with the typical "eat healthy, exercise, don't drink, don't smoke" prescriptions. Instead, for her, it's a matter of commitment.

"The reason I get out of bed in the morning is because I'm able to," she says. "If I can possibly do it, I will do it. It's part of what I promised."

She made the promise back in 1919 when she committed herself to the Benedictine community.

Regina Heyl was a teenager when she heard the calling. She had dropped out of school in eighth grade to work at the H. J. Heinz factory, labeling ketchup bottles. It was good work. And the family needed the money—her father had died when Regina was just five years old.

"My mother had a hard life," she says. In all, her mother had seven children, six girls and a boy. Five of the girls died of childhood diseases before reaching the age of four, so there were just two left, Regina and her baby brother, Hilary. They lived in a small house on Pittsburgh's north side, where Regina's mother raised the children as a single mom

with the help of the church, the neighbors, the community.

"She did housework for people," Sister Regina recalls. "Washing and cleaning and whatever people needed. She worked hard. And she always worked for the sisters."

The same neighborhood sisters who taught Regina encouraged her. The same sisters Regina wondered about, long after she left Sister Seraphim's eighth-grade class.

Sister Seraphim inspired her. She told her she could be anything she wanted to be.

When Regina told her mother what she wanted to be, her mother wondered how the family would survive without the money her daughter was bringing in.

"It was a sacrifice for her," recalls Regina. "Because by that time I had gotten an even better job at a plumbing company. But she was satisfied with my decision. She helped to make all the arrangements."

At seventeen Regina packed her few belongings and stepped into the convent on Canal Street. Five years later, in 1924, she made her final vows. "You felt that was your life," she says. "You felt that was what God wanted you to be, so that's what you became."

It may have been unusual for women to complete high school, much less go to college and graduate school in the 1920s and 1930s, but it was not unusual for nuns. Part of her duty as a sister was to teach, and teachers needed to be educated; Sister Regina's gift for academics was encouraged and allowed to flourish. Soon she was to begin a forty-two-

"THE REASON I GET OUT OF BED IN THE MORNING IS BECAUSE I AM ABLE TO," says Sister Regina Heyl, a member of a Pittsburgh monastery for Benedictine nuns (p. 67) who made her final vows when she was twenty-two (p. 68). As a "whirlwind" teacher at an all-girls school, she can't remember a single discipline problem (above). "It's a changing world," says Sister Regina, with a friend (p. 71). "It was stricter in the early days. Simpler, you know."

year teaching stint at St. Benedict Academy, an all-girls Catholic school attached to the monastery where she was to live for the rest of her life. She never had problems disciplining her students, and can't quite understand the difficulties today regarding disorder in schools.

"I had students who wanted to study," she says. "They wanted to be there. That really made a big difference."

Not so, says Sister Roberta Campbell, class of 1960, who was no fan of algebra. A former student of Sister Regina's, at fifty-five she is one of the youngest nuns at the monastery, and the current prioress, or mother superior. She wears a flower-print shirt and slacks, in contrast to Sister Regina's traditional habit. She has no idea just how many nuns at the monastery are Regina's former students. "Probably most of us," she says. "She inspired a lot of women."

She tells of the "whirlwind" nun who would dash into class with chalk dust all over her veil and habit. "In the name of the Father and of the Son and of the Holy Spirit, direct we beseech thee, Oh, Lord," Sister Regina would begin, and as soon as prayer was over, before anyone had the chance to open a book, she'd call the first row to the board. "And if you were making the stupidest mistake she'd come over and say, 'Now, you don't really mean twenty-three here, do you?'" recalls Sister Roberta. "And you'd say, 'Well, no.' And she'd say, 'I bet if you try thirty-four, now try thirty-four and see if that doesn't work out.'

"No one was ever made to feel stupid or like they couldn't do it. She never put anybody down."

Not so, says Sister Regina. "I tried not to. But I don't know that I never did."

"Well, you say your students were always the ones who wanted to work hard," says Sister Roberta. "That was because of you. You made us want to."

Sister Regina shrugs, smiles, and looks down. She does not take compliments easily.

In 1985 St. Benedict's Academy closed, forcing Sister Regina into retirement at age eighty-five. Such was the fate of Catholic schools all over America, beginning in the late 1970s. Vocations were shrinking—at its peak in 1960 there were 200 nuns at the monastery—and the cost of hiring lay teachers was growing. (Currently there are about 87,000 nuns in America; in 1960, there were more than 168,000. Just 3 percent of today's nuns are under the age of forty.)

This trend is perhaps Sister Regina's biggest worry in life. "I wish I knew the answer. God has to put the seed there." And if a young woman were to ask her about becoming a sister, she would not employ any fancy powers of persuasion. "I would say, 'Come and see. Come and see for yourself.'"

Today the old St. Benedict Academy building has a new life; the sisters have turned it into a social service center for the aged, and for women in need. The top two floors have been converted into sixteen apartments for victims of domestic abuse.

"It's a changing world," says Sister Regina. "It was stricter in the early days. Simpler, you know. You just did what the Church wanted you to do." But the Church seems to have lost some of its authority. "There's less Catholic religion. It's just a different world."

A world that is not as good as it once was?

She considers this. She struggles with this. "I hate to judge," she says. "I really hate to judge. Um. What do you think?" she says, dumping the difficult question in Sister Roberta's lap.

"I think I never heard an unkind word come out of your mouth," she says.

Sister Regina buries her chin and smiles again.

One thing that Sister Regina says has not changed about the world in the last century—not so much as budged—is the essentials of Benedictine monastic life. And so neither has her commitment to it.

Seventy-eight years ago she made the pledge. In addition to the vows of poverty and celibacy common to all Roman Catholic orders, a Benedictine sister makes other promises, including the important vow of "conversion." This means that she promises to live each and every day to the best of her abilities.

Nowadays, for Sister Regina, that means getting up, getting dressed, putting the butter out, and fixing the jellies just so.

MINNIE LITTLEBEAR

A Forgotten American

Born c. 1897

Minnie Littlebear was born 102 years ago in a wigwam in the woods of
Nebraska. She doesn't mark the passage of time according to a monthly calendar.
Instead, each spring she waits for a desert weed along the side of the road to
begin changing color.

"And on the day it turns to the color of wheat, that's my birthday," she says,
flashing an enormous grin. She is a tall woman with wide eyes, long gray hair,
and deep, plentiful wrinkles.

The daughter of George Greywolf and Mary Bear, Minnie knows little
English. She speaks through an Indian translator, here at a nursing home just
outside the Winnebago reservation in the northeast corner of the state. (Like a
number of her peers, Minnie prefers to be called Winnebago or Indian rather
than Native American; anyone born in America, after all, is a Native American.)

Some of the concepts of the Winnebago, a nation of some four thousand people in Nebraska and another five thousand in Wisconsin, are hard to translate.
For instance, there is the manner in which Minnie's father died. The legend, to
her, is not a particularly strange piece of family lore:

"There was another woman who loved him," she says. "But he already had a
wife and family. Still, this woman was very angry that she could not have him.
So somehow she got a piece of his hair. And with that hair she had a hold on
him." The scorned lover was able to cast a spell on Minnie's father with that

hair. "And eventually, he got sick," she says. "He got a sore on his head. And worms got in. And he got headaches. And then he died."

He died just before Minnie was born. According to Winnebago tradition, a child who never knew her father must be treated with great respect. The youngest of six girls, Minnie was lavished with gifts by the tribe: She received special buckskin clothes and beads and fancy jewelry that she would wear to powwows and harvest celebrations.

Minnie's mother eventually remarried. Her stepfather, Charles French (a Winnebago given an Anglo name by white settlers), built a new log cabin by the river for the family. Minnie was happy. "We had a swing that we hung off a tree. And I would swing and swing and swing." Like her sisters, she did not go to school. The custom was for mothers to teach their children to cook and clean and sew and do beadwork, and fathers to teach their sons how to hunt and be warriors.

When Minnie became a teenager in 1910, something startling happened. "The white man came," she says. "And took me to a boarding school far away."

Boarding school for Indians was a national policy adopted in 1879 that would continue, in various forms, until the 1950s. In its original conception, the idea was to assimilate Indians into mainstream American culture—by force. School-age kids were taken from their families and sent sometimes hundreds of miles away to government-run schools. Once there, a child's native clothes would be taken away and she would be given a uniform to wear. She would have to wear strange things on her feet called "shoes." Her hair would be cut. She would be forbidden to speak her native language. She would be punished for dancing or practicing Indian traditions. She would not be allowed to speak to her relatives.

Many Indians recall their days in boarding schools as horrific times of forced labor, abuse, and molestation. They blame boarding schools for the breakdown of the Indian family because it forced so many Indians to grow up outside a family structure, with virtually no examples of parenting to imitate when they became parents. Others see the schools as having been the only chance to learn how to read and write, or, at the

very least, as places that provided meals and shelter, which may have been scarce back on the reservation.

"I missed my mother," Minnie says, remembering little else about her time at the school, which she attended for just two years. (Because her family lived in the woods, it's likely that the government did not know about Minnie's family until Minnie's teenage years. Her older sisters were never sent to the schools.)

Not long after returning from boarding school, Minnie was once again sent away from home. But this time it was to a new home, that of Dave Littlebear. She would be his wife. "One morning mother came and she was with her friend," recalls Minnie. "And she told me, 'This lady has come after you because you're going to be for his son.'" Minnie had no say in the arrangement.

"Three horses, a buggy, a harness, and some shawls," recalls Minnie of the exchange. "That's what my mother got."

There was no wedding. Minnie simply moved that afternoon into Dave's home and waited for him to return from his day of working as a woodsman.

Did she like him?

"He liked me," she says.

Did she think he was handsome?

"No."

Fortunately, Minnie had brought along her cousin that first day. Her cousin stayed with her through the night; Dave slept in another room.

Minnie was not allowed to bring her beautiful clothes and jewelry with her into her marriage. She was part of Littlebear's family now. Unlike the Navajo and other tribes, which are matrilineal, the Winnebago are patrilineal. The man of the family is the boss, and a woman's job is to obey him.

The struggle to make a living would be a constant in Minnie's and Dave's lives, as it was for most Indians. The cooperative structure of Indian society had broken down,

WINNEBAGO MINNIE LITTLEBEAR HOLDS HER SLEEPING GRANDSON ON THE Nebraska reservation she has called home for some 102 years (p. 72). A teenage Minnie (*right*) with a friend before a celebratory dance (p. 75).

thanks to the white man's tinkering. Between 1887 and 1934, in a further attempt to assimilate Indians into white culture, the U.S. government divided up reservations, allotting property to each person on the tribal rolls, and leaving the rest open for homesteading. White settlers flooded onto surplus lands. Indians were forced to move onto widely scattered allotments—leaving them to fend for themselves in a white man's world.

Minnie and her husband made and sold corn liquor, killed and plucked chickens, and in summers headed north to a theme park in Wisconsin that featured Indian wares.

"You could sit out there and do your beadwork and make blankets," Minnie says. "And the white people would come and buy your stuff."

Minnie had a son who died when he was just nine months old. But she raised two other children—Esther, her husband's grandniece, and Barry, who, when his father died, was given to Dave and Minnie. "Because of the wishes of the father, the mother had to let the child go," says Minnie.

Minnie's husband died in the 1970s. Tradition calls for the widow to mourn for four years. Minnie had to wear black, she had to wear shoes instead of going barefoot, and she could not go to powwows or other celebrations. However, in a ritual of dressing and grooming, a Winnebago woman could be "released" from her mourning period early by the women in her deceased husband's family.

"One day my sister-in-law came down and said, 'I'm going to dress you and set you free.'" But Minnie did not want to be free. She liked no longer having to answer to a man. So she stayed in mourning for the full four years.

Esther and other relatives would take care of Minnie for many years on the reservation, until Minnie needed specialized care. Barry, sixty, lives in Black River Falls, Wisconsin, and is a caseworker for senior citizens of the tribe. Esther, fifty-two, lives near her mother and works at the Winna Vegas casino, which is owned and operated by the Winnebago. Many tribes have opened gambling establishments in an attempt to raise revenue. Indians are the poorest racial group in America. Though the national poverty rate stands at 13 percent, for Indians it's 31 percent. One out of every five Indian homes lacks both a telephone and an indoor toilet. More than a third of all Indian students drop out of high school. Indians lead the nation in suicide and in other deaths due to alcoholism, diabetes, and heart disease.

And yet Indians today are asserting their centuries-old right of self-government, becoming increasingly powerful politically at the dawn of the new millennium. For her part, Minnie is not one to complain about the difficult times she has seen her nation experience in the twentieth century. But the word "nation" to her means Winnebago, not the United States of America.

Does Minnie consider herself an American?

Her translator, Betty Greencrow, looks perplexed. She is not sure how to phrase this question in the Winnebago language. "In what sense?" she asks. "You mean in the sense of the American dream? We don't have anything like that."

She thinks some more, but eventually comes up blank. "The conflict is not between Indians and Americans," she explains. "It's between Indians and white people. Being an American doesn't mean anything."

Does Minnie feel angry at white people?

Greencrow is able to pose that question to Minnie.

"There is some resentment," Minnie says, ashamed. Anger is not the Winnebago way. She does not, however, believe that the white man is evil.

"He is greedy," she says.

ROSE KOTZ

Surviving the Sweatshops

Born 1903

At Bowler City in Hackensack, New Jersey, it's the Air Balls versus Rose's Girls. Team captain Rose Kotz, ninety-five, has just arrived. She's about five decades older than most of these other bowlers, a tiny woman, just four feet seven, with auburn hair that never went gray.

"Hey, Rosie!" says a teammate. "You gonna bowl two twenty-one today?" It was Rose's highest score, which she got back when she was ninety-two. Her average is a more modest hundred.

"I don't know," she says. She's not feeling well. "I tell you, this morning I didn't think I had enough energy to walk." She opens her locker, looks inside, pokes around with her cane. She hooks it onto the handle of her bowling-ball bag. One good yank and the eight-pounder falls to the floor with a thud. She drags the ball the length of the bowling alley toward lane eleven, chattering away in the thick Austrian accent that is distinctly hers.

"You see this bag?" she says. "I made this bag. You see this apron I'm wearing? I made this apron. You see these trousers? I made them. Everything you see, I made. I made my coats. I made my shawls. I made fifty-one shawls and gave them all away. It's the truth, so I can say it. You ask, 'Why did you give away fifty-one shawls?' Well, it's me. You see it. You like it. I give it to you."

Rose made her way in the world working as a seamstress in the garment factories of New York and New Jersey, joining many turn-of-the-century Eastern European immigrants. But Rose was born in America. It was her identity, her blood, her pride. She was the oldest of six children born in Massachusetts. As babies, she and a sister were sent to live with their grandmother in Austria. Rose had three and a half years of formal schooling, then learned sewing from her cousins. She did not know how to read or write when she returned to America, a dream come true, at nineteen. In America anything was possible. She moved in with an aunt and got a job in a factory sewing ladies' clothes.

"And I got the newspaper every day," she says. "I taught myself to read by getting the newspaper. And did you know the seventeenth president of the United States never went

one day to school? He didn't know how to read or write until his girlfriend taught him. And he became a president. That's what can happen in America

"What? I'm up? It's my turn? All right." She stands. She grabs hold of her red ball with both hands, saunters with some difficulty up to the line. She doesn't so much throw the ball as drop it, giving it a little forward push. She turns, faces her friends.

"What did I make—did I get anything down?" she asks.
"The ball's not quite there yet, Rose. Hang on."
The ball gradually reaches the pins, and five of them tumble.
"Five, Rosie. You got five down."
"That's nice," she says. "That makes me feel better. I tell you, this morning I didn't think I could walk."

In the beginning Rose made a dollar a week as a factory seamstress. Salaries for women in the early 1900s in the textile and garment industries, the so-called "needle trades," were often at sweatshop levels. The hours were long and the conditions deplorable. In 1911 a fire broke out at New York City's Triangle Shirtwaist Company factory and 146 employees, most of them young women, burned to death because there were no usable emergency exits.

Unions changed all of that. In 1914 Congress passed the Clayton Act, which guaranteed workers the right to unionize, strike, boycott, and picket. But unions did not become a force until the 1930s, when President Franklin D. Roosevelt's New Deal policies caused a surge in union membership. A national Social Security program was established, along with unemployment compensation, worker's compensation, and a federal minimum-wage law. (The original minimum hourly pay set in 1938 was twenty-five cents per hour.)

Rose will tell you that Roosevelt changed her life. She

SHE MAY BE FIVE DECADES OLDER THAN HER COMPANIONS, BUT ROSE KOTZ IS team captain of Rose's Girls at Bowler City in Hackensack, New Jersey (p. 76). Pictured with a friend (p. 77), Rose worked as a garment-factory seamstress when she was a young woman. Though born in America, she spent her childhood in Austria (p. 79). Rose, whose bowling average is 100, goes for a strike (p. 80).

went from earning a dollar a week to nine dollars and then to nineteen dollars. "And he made it so we had five-day weeks, seven hours a day," she recalls. "And if you worked more than that, you got even more money. Overtime, they called it. One time I made seventy-two dollars in one week! It's the truth, so I can say it . . .

"What? I'm up? Again?" Well, actually, she has not yet completed the frame.

She stands, gets her trusty red ball, repeats her technique. "What did I make? Did I make anything?"

"A spare!" shouts a teammate. "Rosie, you got a spare!"

"It's good," she says. "This morning, I tell you, I thought if I don't end up in the hospital, it will be a miracle."

Rose used to wonder why her husband, who worked as a baker, never had any money. Alfred was a German immigrant whom Rose married when she was twenty-eight. They lived in a small house in Fort Lee, New Jersey. "I'd give my husband money to buy himself a pair of shoes," she says. "And he'd come home without the shoes, without the money." It kept happening.

One day there was a knock at the door. It was the FBI.

"Where's your husband?" the agent said.

"He's at work," she said.

"How many meetings have you attended?" he said.

"What?"

Rose was forty-one. She was dumbfounded to learn from the FBI agents that her husband of thirteen years was a Nazi, a member of the German-American Bund. That's where all the money went, to a loosely organized group of some 25,000 people, most of them German immigrants who followed Adolf Hitler and were determined to "cleanse" America of the Jews and other minorities, just as Hitler was cleansing Germany.

The year was 1944. The United States and its allied forces were preparing for D-Day, the invasion of Europe, the most massive military operation in American history. Enemy sympathizers would not be tolerated on U.S. soil. Rose's husband was arrested, and eventually deported. "And he told me to come with him," she recalls. "He said, 'Pack the trunk, lock the house, come with me.'"

"I said, 'Are you crazy!?' I got a divorce. I got my maiden name back. I never spoke to him again."

And so Rose supported herself with her sewing. "And I tell you the truth, the house, when he left, it wasn't a house. It was a shack. No gas. No water in it. There was water outside. And I made a house out of it. I did everything. I'm a painter. I'm a plumber. I'm a carpenter. I'm everything. You know what I mean? I'm American born. I can do anything."

Rose retired at sixty-five. "I'm sorry, yes, I did. I should not have." Her Social Security checks are a mere five hundred dollars a month. She sold the house and moved into a low-income assisted-living home for senior citizens.

"Nothing to brag about," Rose says about her home. "There's nothing to do there. Once a week a bingo. That's all. I hate to say it, but it's true."

This is why Rose thanks God, and the Blessed Mother she wears on a chain around her neck, for the bowlers. She's played in Monday and Wednesday leagues ever since she was seventy-two and discovered bowling. She is less interested in her bowling technique—she can barely see the pins—than she is in the other bowlers.

"If there wouldn't be the bowlers," she says, "I wouldn't be where I am today." The bowlers pick her up, take her home. The bowlers drop by with flowers. The bowlers shop for her. The bowlers call her each morning, make sure she's okay. The bowlers are her family.

Today Rose's Girls beat the Air Balls three games to two.

"That's good," says Rose. "So let's eat." They head to the snack bar. "I'll have the chicken fingers and vegetables. Now you girls go put in your orders." The women come back with burgers and curly fries and Cokes. Rose stands up to pay. It is very important to her that she treat. It is a gift she knows she can't afford, but every week she somehow manages to. She hands the cashier a twenty. The cashier pretends to put the money in the register, but instead slips it to a waiting bowler, who slips it back into Rose's purse. They do this every week.

"Thanks for lunch, Rosie," they'll say, around the table, one by one. "Thanks, Rose."

"You are welcome," she'll say. "You are welcome."

bess hoffman

The Day the Earth Shook

___

Born 1897

Bess Brodofsky was ten years old, a self-described "husky girl" who loved to munch on the chocolate for sale in her mother's general store on the outskirts of San Francisco. At about five A.M. on the morning of April 18, 1906, she was awakened suddenly. Was this a dream? What was happen-

ing? The glass pitcher on the shelf above her bed fell to the floor. Two glasses followed, then six more.

The San Francisco earthquake, arguably the worst natural disaster in American history, had hit.

"I get chills when I think about it," says Bess, now 102, sitting safe and secure in the activities room at the Jewish Home for the Aged in San Francisco. The memories flash before her, images that appear in no particular order. "I remember the children, naked children," she says. "And my father throwing down his crutches. And my mother, she let the people in and fed them."

Chaos is her only sure memory. The quake itself lasted just forty-eight seconds, and was felt from Oregon to southern California and as far east as central Nevada. The region of destruction extended about 400 miles, with the city of San Francisco its bull's-eye. Buildings collapsed and hundreds died as the ground liquefied beneath them. Most of the buildings caught fire—a fire that lasted four days. Three fourths of the city burned to the ground. Some twenty thousand people were picked up by the U.S.S. *Chicago* in the largest evacuation by sea in history. Others fled to parks, to the countryside, and to other safe places.

Bess's neighborhood on San Bruno Avenue south of the city was one such haven. "We were not hurt. Our homes were still standing," she says. But her grandparents and other family members were in the city, somewhere in the fire zone. Bess will never forget what her father did. He was a feeble man, confined to a life with crutches due to an arthritic condition that had brought the family to the warm California climate from Winnipeg, Canada.

"When he heard about the fire," recalls Bess, "my father threw down his crutches. And he jumped in the wagon to go get his family out of that fire. He drove the horse into San Francisco and rescued the family. And it was never explained to me why, but he never used his crutches again after that."

Even more vividly, Bess remembers her mother's heroics during the great fire. "She emptied the store," she says. "She gave all the people clothes, food, anything from the store that they wanted. The people kept coming up from the fire. And the children were naked. The fire had burned their clothes right off them. My mother dressed them.

"And when the baker came in the morning, she took every loaf that he had. And she sent me out to the one-legged man that sold eggs. I bought all his eggs. And so we served all the people breakfast."

Bess and her mother knew how to work as a team. The oldest daughter, Bess had already delivered a few of her mother's babies. "In that time we didn't have doctors available," she says. "It was just my mother and me. She would tell me what to do and I would do it. She'd say, 'Put more hot water on! Bring more of the hot water!' And 'Keep the kettle going!'

"Mostly it went okay. But I remember one of the babies I delivered did die. It was born alive. I was supposed to take care of it. And people claimed I didn't do it right. I don't

know. I was seven years old." In all, Bess would deliver six of her siblings successfully.

Bess went to grade school while also holding down a job at a dime store for six dollars a month, thus helping her mother to feed the family. Her father's arthritic condition kept him from ever working. Bess maintained other jobs while keeping up her studies through the eighth grade. She did not like school. "I didn't have many friends," she says. "A lot of the kids were terrible. They'd pull your hair and call you 'Icky' or 'Sheeny' or things like that because we were Jewish.

"And we had a terrible principal, too. Miss Kessner. If we were late for school or if we took a day off for a Jewish holiday, she would slap our hands with a ruler for hours.

"She was really terrible."

Bess loved to dance. "Three-step, two-step, one-step, I loved them all," she says. "I would go very often dancing. But my mother would always come along." A chaperone was part of the dating tradition of the day. "If you went on a picnic with a boy, your mother came along."

Bess would not know true happiness until she was in her twenties. It came in the form of one Louis Hoffman. They were introduced through a mutual acquaintance. "I was in love with him right away," she says with a giggle in her voice and the look of a rascal in her eye.

He was a would-be inventor who was working on an unsinkable ship and a prototype for the monkey wrench. And he was making his living in a salvage business with his brother. "They would go about the city and they would yell, 'Rags! Bottles! Sacks!' They went around buying trash and odd things from people and would turn it around and sell it.'"

But when Bess met him he hardly had the look of a junk dealer. He wore spats and fancy shoes. "Oh, he was all dressed up. He was just like a king. He asked me on a date. And I said, 'Can I bring my sister along?' And he said, 'Bring whoever you like!'"

They went for a car ride, and two years later they married, and then had two children. They settled in San

"I GET CHILLS WHEN I THINK ABOUT IT," SAYS BESS HOFFMAN (P. 83) of the 1906 San Francisco earthquake that convulsed her life when she was ten. A would-be inventor named Louis Hoffman who wore spats captured her heart; she married him (p. 82) and settled in a recovering San Francisco. "I was in love with him right away," she says today (p. 85).

Francisco, a city still reinventing itself more than a decade after the devastating quake. Louis became a successful cabinetmaker, with his own store.

Bess never forgot the example of caregiving that she received from her mother during that time of chaos and ruin. She assumed a maternal role with all her brothers and sisters throughout her life, and was always active in volunteering in hospitals and charitable organizations.

"Most of her life was spent really being a caregiver for other people who needed her," says her daughter, Miriam Wain, now seventy-seven. "She was always running with the soup, the chicken soup. But she was never there when I came home from school. She was too busy helping others."

Miriam felt left out and resentful. She held a grudge against her mother for many years. It was much later in life, when Miriam was forced to take on the role of nurturer, that the two would forge a lasting relationship.

"My father died in the 1960s," says Miriam. "And in the last few years my mother needed me. And a miracle happened when I started caring for her. I realized I really loved her. It's just something about the act of taking care of another person that makes you open your heart."

It's just something that was passed down, woman to woman, through three generations.

martha
jane
faulkner

Coming to the Promised Land

———————

Born 1894

"The projects," says Martha Jane Faulkner, 104, "they call this the projects where I live." The windows are locked shut here in her tiny apartment in one of Newark, New Jersey's poorest sections. The air is stale and the neighbors are loud. And yet Martha is remarkably at peace here.

"Yeah, it's nice," she says. "You can see it's nice." She has, after all, only one flight of steps to climb when she comes home. She lives here with her grand-daughter, Mary Stacey, fifty-seven.

"And I can get around the whole house," she says. "In the morning I can go in there and fix me a cup of coffee, fix my cereal and eat it. And I have a tele-phone right next to me here. The only thing is, I don't have a washing machine. But that's all right."

For some sixty years she worked as a cleaning woman for wealthy white fami-lies in New York City's bedroom communities. When Martha was in her twen-ties, she moved here from the South, the migration pattern of thousands of African Americans, and the story of twentieth-century urban America that did not often have a happily-ever-after ending.

Martha was born on a farm near Halifax, Virginia. "My father was in slavery until he was fifteen," she says. "He used to tell me stories about it. In slavery

they didn't pay the coloreds nothing. But when he got out of slavery, he got paid."

As a girl Martha worked on a farm with her father, two brothers, and a sister. Her mother had died when she was just two. "I was the baby child," she says. "And we planted corn and tobacco and wheat. We didn't never bother with cotton. Tobacco was our main article. You sorted the leaves off the stalk and you had to cut it, and after you cut it you had to cure it until it got dry."

Martha began school at age seven, and continued through the eighth grade. "I will never forget," she says, "it could be raining, pouring rain, and my father would get that old horse and buggy and he'd come after me. Yes, he would, to keep me from plowing home from school in the rain. I thank him for that. Oh, he was a good father."

Martha continued working on the farm until she was nineteen and married David Faulkner. He wanted a better life for his family; he wanted to pursue the American Dream in the cities of the North. In 1917 he and Martha, who by now had two children, Irene and James, came north.

Newark was a thriving industrialized center that encouraged the migration of southern blacks as a source of labor. European immigration, the previous source of labor, had been virtually choked off by World War I. Between 1910 and 1920, the number of black residents rose from 9,475 to 16,977. The city was not, by all accounts, ready for such a huge population influx. A severe housing shortage combined with a predominantly white middle class that held prejudice against southern blacks helped set the stage for decades of racial strife.

Most newcomers were forced to find residence in the central part of the city, the so-called Hill districts, which became the center of a ghetto. Poor conditions threatened their health. In 1919 the death rate for Newark blacks was twice that of whites.

Jobs at this time were, however, plentiful. David got a good job with a construction company, which he would hold for most of his life. Martha worked for nearly two years in a shipyard, cleaning ships.

"But my work after that was always the Misses work,"

she says, "washing and ironing and cleaning." She worked mainly for three families, and is as proud as a sports hero to announce her statistics: "forty-three, twelve and twenty-three," she says, referring to the number of the years she worked for each family.

She took three buses and a taxi to get to Yvonne Patterson's house in Watchung, New Jersey, every Friday. She was paid $10 for a day's work there, plus travel expenses. She cleaned, did laundry, ironed shirts, and made the evening meal. And she did a lot more than that. She took care of the puppies, spent pleasant afternoons with Yvonne, and passed on words of wisdom. She became a part of the family.

One time Yvonne decided to pay Martha a visit in her home in the projects. As she was getting out of her car, a white policeman stopped her to ask where she was going. When she told him she was going to visit an old friend, he told her to lock the car, go in, and not to stay more than five minutes. It was broad daylight.

As in so many northern cities, racial tensions in Newark had increased to the point of violence. In 1967 the infamous Newark riots broke out. By this time nearly 200,000 blacks lived in housing projects in the century-old slums of Central Ward, many of these homes without heat or hot water. The factories had closed and jobs were now scarce. White politicians still controlled a mostly black city. Poor housing, limited economic advancement, and white indifference created a pressure cooker that finally blew its lid on a hot July after-

IN 1917, MARTHA JANE FAULKNER SAID GOOD-BYE TO FARMING IN VIRGINIA and moved with her husband and children to Newark, New Jersey, where she (pp. 86 and 89) worked as a maid "washing and ironing and cleaning" until she was eighty-seven. When she turned 100, her church gave her a trophy.

noon. Five days of violence ended with two dozen dead.

As for Martha, she was either insulated from the effects of the violence or she chooses to avoid it when she looks back on her life. Instead, she thinks about her husband, her kids, and her extended family, which included her employers. The last family she worked for, the Menckes, so considered her a part of their family that when little Johnny Mencke got married, he had Martha picked up in a limo and taken to the wedding. She sat at the head table.

Martha was eighty-seven when she quit working as a maid, due to the difficulty she was having with her legs. Her husband had died seven years previously, when he was eighty-five. "We had a very satisfied life," she says. "Now, don't think we didn't raise hell. But we did stuff together. I

never was a person who went to a tavern. But sometimes he would want to. So he'd bring me home first. And he'd go back. I didn't care, because I could trust him. We were together fifty-nine years before he passed."

Both of her children are also deceased now, but she has a few grandchildren left to look after her, and to stop over for a mean game of pinochle. "It's a fact that nobody can win pinochle over me," she says. Several of Martha's previous employers, and their children, whom Martha helped raise, are still in Martha's life. Now scattered across the country, they call her often.

"I have my telephone here," she says. "They call me. They tell me, they say, 'I'm not going to forget you as long as you live.' So that shows my work was worth something. They remember me with a halo on."

emma washa

Reporting from the Prairie

Born 1896

In the weekly column she has been writing for the *Boscobel Dial* for the past three decades, Emma Washa, 101, chronicles life as she knows it from her Wisconsin home. She writes about snow, tractors, geese, and the good old days on the prairie, where she raised her nine kids, milked thirteen cows twice a day, and ran a general store.

"Oh, it would take me a week to tell you all that I've been through," she says, sitting in the tidy Castle Rock, Wisconsin, home where she lives alone. A card table in the corner of the living room doubles as her desk and is where she writes "Observations" in longhand. In another corner is her bed, with a curtain around it. She wears a pretty flowered dress and a tight white perm.

"I was born just over the ridge," she says, explaining that her father was the son of pioneers. As a little girl, Emma

loved to listen to his tales of sailing from Bohemia (now a region of the Czech Republic) to the New World in a two-week journey filled with storms and mermaids' songs. The family headed to North Dakota, where it staked its claim and built a sod shanty. The winds were high and water was scarce. Forced to find a better life, Emma's father eventually settled on more fertile land in Wisconsin and raised his family there. Emma worked the farm. She remembers driving the cows down to pasture while riding Flory, her horse. She remembers whacking a bull on the head with a stick one morning to save her father from being gouged. She remembers nights as cold as forty degrees below zero, when the woodstove was unable to keep up. She remembers the quilts she made from the family's chicken feathers.

And she remembers her father's newspaper column. He

wrote about local events, including who had the preacher over to dinner and what kind of potatoes were served—coverage that was typical in rural newspapers at the turn of the century. By the time Emma was eight, he had tired of the job and turned it over to her.

"Back then, reporting was a lot easier," she says, recalling how early telephone lines were shared by whole communities. "We had over twenty people on our same phone line. So you could just lift the receiver and listen to what was going on. You know, maybe somebody went to town and got a hundred pounds of sugar for canning. Maybe somebody was having roast beef for dinner. You would just go and write it all down."

But Emma never had her sights set on any sort of career—an anathema to the rough-and-tumble life that filled her landscape; she had her sights set on a certain fellow. His name was Frank Washa and he was eleven years older than she. When she was sixteen, she finally got up the nerve to ask him to dance at a church social.

"And one day he asked me to kiss him," she recalls. She declined. "I said, 'Well, I read an article that says you should never kiss until you're engaged.' He mumbled something to himself and went away. And I thought, 'Oh no! What did I do? You know, that's the end of that.' But it wasn't. The next day he came over. He said, 'I want you for my wife.'"

Emma and Frank were married in a snowstorm in February 1915. Emma's father went ahead of the bride in a bobsled pulled by the team of horses, clearing the snow with a shovel and eventually cutting through a neighbor's fence to get Emma to the church on time. She wore a shoe-top-length dress of gray silk mousseline and white shoes with eight buttons. She had a

dowry: a feather comforter, a couple of wool blankets, four sets of sheets, and two pillows. After the ceremony, at a dinner in their house, Emma's parents gave the newlyweds their wedding present: a cow.

Emma and Frank settled in a log house on a small farm. "There were two rooms downstairs and two attic rooms," she recalls. And soon there were three babies. And no electricity, no refrigeration, or gas. Emma took care of the children and helped Frank with the farm. Thirteen cows had to be milked twice a day. Emma worked fast to finish six before Frank did. "So I would get the thirteenth cow," she says. "Because I didn't want Frank to have to do it. I tried to save him as much as I could." She went on to have six more children. All—like her first three—were born at home.

Eventually, the family moved into town. They ran a general store out of the first floor of their house. Emma was now the mother of nine, as well as the manager of the store. Frank worked as a blacksmith and manufactured hundreds of gallons of sorghum a year. It seemed like everything was going perfectly for the Washas—until that day in 1940 when fire broke out in a side room. The Fennimore Fire Department rushed to the scene, but its pumps were frozen in the December air. "So we stood there and watched our lives burn to the ground," recalls Emma. They hadn't been able to afford insurance.

They moved to a ten-by-twenty-foot cabin, fully expecting to rebuild the store. "But then they took our boys to the service," she says. Three of Emma's sons served their country in World War II. "You never knew if your kids were going to come home," she says. She remembers the waiting. She will never forget the waiting. "And we always said we would rebuild the store if they came home," she says. "So we stayed in that cabin, waiting. And it got so cold. We had boxes stuck under the bed, you know, to make more room. And we tried to pull those boxes out, but they were frozen to the floor."

Desperate for warmth—and money—Emma and Frank moved to the city of Madison, Wisconsin. Both got jobs at the Oscar Mayer meat-processing plant, back when Oscar himself ran things. They took other jobs, too— Frank during the day, and Emma at night. Emma put tops on batteries at Ray-O-Vac. She manufactured hand grenades at Madison Kipp. She drove a cab.

"You did what you had to do," she says. "You didn't think about it. You had to find a way to make money."

Her sons came home alive from the war, although one was a lot worse for the wear. "His work was in the hospital," she says. "The soldiers came in wounded. Some of them were lonesome and crying for their wives. And they went nuts. The war made them crazy. So my son, his job was to hold them down in bed. He'd kneel on them to hold them down."

"He was never the same after that." Years later, that same son would die of a brain tumor. Emma blamed the war. She can't prove it, but Emma believes the madness of war can bring cancer to a man.

Emma and Frank did eventually rebuild the house that was the general store. It is the house that Emma lives in today. Frank died in 1972, at age eighty-six. Emma is surrounded by photographs of her nine children, fifty-five grandchildren, one hundred and nine great-grandchildren, and eight great-great-grandchildren, a number of whom live close enough that there is always a family member checking on her. While all of Emma's children had family farms, only one of the fifty-five grandchildren does. "It's the modern times, you know—money. Today, farmers can barely make a living, and the family farm is dying."

She is happy here. She is not one to dwell on the hardships of her past. At least not unless there is a lesson to be learned. She remembers a fall she took when she was sixty-five, heading out for a drive in her Maverick. She fell in the snow and slid under her car, fracturing her hip. A lot of people might see that as a reason to cave in. But not Emma. She was too busy being impressed by the local rescue squad who came and saved her. She was so grateful to them she wrote a thank-you note in the form of a letter to the editor of the *Dial*. She wrote another letter thanking her friends for all the pies and cookies they brought during her recuperation. "And little by little, that's how the column started," she says. "I just kept writing to the paper." She has been writing the column for more than thirty-five years. It is, she allows, the thing that keeps her alive. "It is good for my brain."

Even so, it is hard to do. When you are 101 years old, it is hard to produce twenty inches of copy every week. "It would be easy to quit," she says. "Very easy." But she won't. She has things to share with her readers.Important things. In a recent column she tells the story of how birds learned to fly:

"And first they were created without wings," writes Emma. "And then God made wings and set them down before the wingless birds and said, 'Come take up these burdens and bear them.'" The birds were not happy to have to lug around the extra weight. "But soon they learned to use them," writes Emma, "and were lifted by them into the air and from their burdens came wings."

EMMA WASHA STILL FILES HER NEWSPAPER COLUMN FROM HER TIDY WISCONSIN home (p. 90). Emma shows off a 4½-pound trout in the early 1940s (p. 91). Emma looks through old photos, including one of her nine children and some of their cousins (p. 93, *lower left*). A young Emma, flanked by her brother Joe (*right*) and his friend (*left*), peeks from behind the day's catch, circa 1907 (p. 94). Emma (*right*) in a huddle with sister Josephine (*left*) and sister-in-law Kate (*center*) in 1918 (*above*).

hazel wolf

Protecting Mother Earth ❧ Born 1898

Sitting in her Seattle apartment, Hazel Wolf, 100, is working on the keynote speech she will deliver to a gathering of corporate heads from the nation's timber companies.

"Oh, I guess I'll talk to them about sustainable management of forests," she says casually, as if this were the most typical thing in the world for a 100-year-old woman to do. She likes giving speeches. When she was ninety-nine, and receiving an honorary doctorate from Seattle University, she stood before the graduating class and advised the students to remember the words of an ancient Chinese philosopher who said that in order to go one thousand miles, one must take the first step.

"Unfortunately, he or she didn't say what to do next," she said, standing there in her cap and gown, "and so we are left with one foot in the air."

An environmentalist and peace activist, an atheist and former member of the Communist party, Hazel Wolf has spent her eighties and nineties camping, hiking, canoeing—in a forty-foot dugout canoe with Mayan Indian tribes—zipping off to Nicaragua six times to monitor elections there, producing a newsletter for the Federation of Western Outdoor Clubs, and organizing more chapters of the National Audubon Society than any other individual in the association's history.

"I'm kind of street-wise," she says. "I come from poor, working-class people. I look on that—poverty—as one of my most treasured legacies."

She lives by herself on a $795 monthly Social Security check. In her apartment, rickety bookcases hold her cherished classics, and an overturned crate holds her boom box, college-dorm style. She walks and takes buses and bums rides from friends. She has no health insurance, makes all her clothes, and lives on a diet that consists primarily of steamed vegetables. "I don't want a lot of things," she says.

Hazel Wolf was born in Victoria, British Columbia, the oldest of three. Her father, a seaman, died when Hazel was just six, leaving her mother penniless. Her mother got a job in an overalls factory, and Hazel remembers going with her to union meetings.

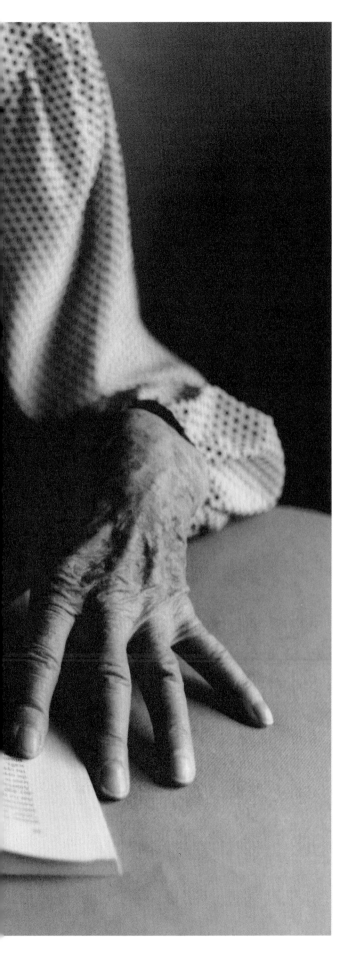

"I had tremendous energy as a kid," she says, "maybe more than most children." Part tomboy and part bookworm, she remembers the urge to organize. She started the first girls' basketball team in her grade school. "The principal said, 'Girls don't play basketball,' And I said, 'That's because we don't have any basketballs.' He couldn't back out of that one."

Fresh out of eighth grade, Hazel landed a job as a legal secretary. "You didn't need a Ph.D. to work in a law office in those days," she says. She earned $25 a month. The first $15 went to her mother, for board. The next $5 paid for the loan she got to buy herself a bicycle. "And I guess the other $5 I bought candy with or something. I already had a bathing suit."

She married at twenty—an event she chooses not to talk about—and had a daughter. A few years later she moved with her daughter to America. "Just like any other immigrant," she says, "I came for a better job." A single mother, she found work in another law office, but when the Depression hit, she was out of work.

"I went on welfare," she says. "They called it 'relief' back then." She used the free time to get a high school diploma, then a college degree. She zipped through her course work in a matter of two years. "I figured out how to work the system," she allows.

Like thousands of others, during the Depression she went to work for the Work Projects Administration (WPA), which hired the unemployed for public works projects.

It was during this time that Hazel hooked up with the Communist party. "A friend invited me to a meeting," she recalls. "And they were handing out pamphlets, the *Communist Manifesto* by Karl Marx. I still have it. There wasn't a thing in there that I didn't already know from birth. He said the middle class is a buffer between the very rich and the very poor. I hated the middle class. I had no hesitancy in joining."

Party members were active. "We'd take on cases of people who couldn't get on welfare for some screwball reason," she says, "and fight the authorities and get them on. It was a cruel time for people." She began organizing labor unions within the WPA.

Hazel's party membership ended shortly after the United States entered World War II, and she got a job as a legal secretary to a civil rights lawyer. "All the unemployed had jobs, or they were in the armed forces. There were no starving people around." And so, to her, the Communist party simply wasn't any fun anymore. "I'm an active person," she says. "We just sat around talking about raising funds for this and that. I got bored and drifted away."

Her affiliation would come back to haunt her, though, during the McCarthy era. Because she had once been a member of the Communist party, the Federal Immigration and Naturalization Service tried to have her deported as a threat to national security. "Canada-born Secretary Held as Red," the headline read on Memorial Day 1949.

"Yeah, I was thrown in the slammer," she says. "There were a couple of women in the jail," she recalls. "And they said, 'What are you in for?' And I said, 'Well, I've been accused of trying to overthrow the government.' They'd never heard of such a noble crime."

Within a day she was let out on bail. "On the condition that I not leave the country," she says. "Think that one over when you get home."

She was fifty-one years old, and she had not yet even been introduced to the passion that would ignite her for the rest of her life: conservation. She became involved with the Audubon Society in pretty much the same way she did the Communist party: She wandered into a meeting, a favor to a friend. Soon she was being dragged on a bird-watching trip.

"So I was with all these people who were standing there looking at a little bird," she recalls. "And it was going up a tree, *tick, tick, tick*, searching for bugs. I learned later that it was called a brown creeper." She stood there watching the bird for a long time. "And when I saw this little bird doing this all day long, up and down the tree, I saw that that little guy worked hard for a living. I related to that. It had this little lifestyle. And I had a little lifestyle, too. I get up in the morning, eat my breakfast, go to work, have my lunch, go back to work, come home, eat my dinner. I related to that little bird. I thought, Well, we're just soul mates. We both have the same problems."

She would go on to encourage the connection between people and wildlife, in speeches to children as well as corporations, in her work as a tireless crusader for environmental issues. She retired as a legal secretary in 1965, but continues to work for the Seattle Audubon Society.

"I got fifty-five new members last year," she says. "I always carry membership forms in my purse."

Hazel has devoted her time to countless other causes. She has lobbied for federal aid to out-of-work loggers and cofounded a group aimed at alleviating pollution in Seattle's poor neighborhoods. She entered the political thicket of Central American strife when she visited Nicaragua for the first time in 1985, and then campaigned for medical supplies and other aid to this country.

Her apartment walls are lined with plaques and awards for her efforts. She is still collecting more. She plans to keep on working until the day she dies.

She sees no heaven in her own future. She was raised as an atheist, and remains one today. "But I wouldn't lift a finger to convert anybody to atheism," she says. "Because there's absolutely nothing to offer in its place.

"When I die, I want to go back where I came from, back to Mother Earth."

For all her activism, she is not pessimistic about the fate of the environment.

"I'm hopeful about the generations to come," she says. "It's much more fun feeling that way. I believe we'll get together and help each other survive. We crave our fellow human beings. The worst punishment you can give a person is solitary confinement. We just crave to be together. So I don't think we're going to do anything to destroy our habitat. We'll get together and fix it.

"We've got two things, our genes and our culture, both driving us into a brotherhood," she says, then stops to think for a moment. "I don't know what to do about that word. 'Siblinghood?'"

A PASSSIONATE ACTIVIST FOR NUMEROUS SOCIAL CAUSES, HAZEL WOLF (p. 96) STILL makes plenty of public speeches. In her early twenties she moved with her daughter, Nydia (p. 97), from Canada to the United States. "I'm hopeful about the generations to come," says Hazel, still an avid reader (p. 98). As a teenager, Hazel readies for a dip at a swimming club in Victoria, British Columbia (p. 101).

LINA BEACON

The Heroism of an Everyday Housewife

Born 1898

Lina Beacon, ninety-nine, would really like a bite of her sweet roll. But her daughter, Violet, seventy-four, won't give her the chance to stop talking and eat. Neither will her granddaughter, Melissa, forty-four, nor her great-granddaughter Rebecca, sixteen. Three women from three generations sit in the kitchen and fire questions to the woman they call Grandma. They like to hear what it used to be like. How it was to walk your scaredy-cat big sister out to the outhouse in the middle of the night. How it was to wash clothes in a big boiling pot that you stirred with a poker. How it was to wear a bra the year bras were first invented. ("I said, 'I'm not wearing that thing!'") And how it was to be a woman on the sidelines of two world wars: Her husband served in the first one; years later, during the second, her son's ship was blown up by a torpedo.

"And he swam for his life?" says Melissa, just as Lina is about to take a bite.

"I'm not answering till I eat this thing!" she says, and the four women share a laugh.

Lina has lived her whole life on New York's Long Island. She's the daughter of a German immigrant who arrived in 1890 ready to make his mark as a carpenter. Lina was the second child, a pretty girl with long red hair who lived,

thanks to her father's talents, in the most modern home in Hicksville. "We had a pump right there in the kitchen!" she says proudly. "We didn't have to go outside for our water." Lina went to the local German school and learned what girls learned: how to read and write and sew and clean and cook. She graduated from eighth grade with her greatest accomplishment on her back: her homemade graduation dress. At sixteen, she commuted to her first job at the B. Altman department store in New York City by horse-drawn trolley car. She earned twelve dollars a month as a salesclerk; later, Lord & Taylor offered her a one-dollar raise to be a cashier. She would sit in the basement and take the money out of the basket that had traveled all the way through the store via pulleys. She would make change, then send the basket back to the clerk. "They didn't trust too many people with money back then," she says. "But they trusted me."

One day Lina went to a neighborhood dance and met a nice boy, one of the popular "carnation boys." These were a group of young men who delighted in being gentlemen—and always wore carnations in their lapels. One of them—"as handsome as James Cagney"—asked Lina to dance. "But he couldn't dance," she says. "No. Not good. But I liked him. And later I took him home to show my mother. And she said, 'Watch it.' She said, 'You have a good father and a good mother so don't do anything disgraceful.'"

Lina and Jerry went on dates. "Mostly movies," she says. "Open-air movies. The piano man was in a shed and we would climb the ladder and lie on that shed and peek in and see him."

They were in love. And the world was just going to war. In 1917 nationalism was rampant. Men flocked to recruiting stations to sign up. The idea of dying for your country was the essence of manliness. Supporting your man on behalf of your country was a woman's greatest honor.

Lina wanted to marry Jerry before he went off to war. He said no, not yet. "He said he wanted to make sure he came back a whole man," she says. "A lot of men had an arm shot off or a leg, you know. And the girls who were married to them had to keep them. He didn't want that. He didn't want to come back and be a burden."

Lina received regular letters from Jerry, although she never knew where he was; the letters were censored and the names of locations were always the first to be blackened out. Finally, in 1918, the war ended, having cost some 20 million lives.

Jerry came home a whole man with a present for Lina he had picked up in France: an engagement ring. Lina put it on and the two went to church. "And after church we went back to see the minister and we got married." It was Thanksgiving Day, 1919.

Her husband got a clerical job with the New York City Board of Education, and Lina became a homemaker and mother of two—first Gerald, then Violet. Money was tight but there wasn't too much Lina needed to buy. She sewed all the clothes, made all the pillows from the feathers she'd pluck off the chickens in the backyard coop. And it just seemed the world was getting more and more modern. One day running water was put in the house and the next day lightbulbs. Soon there was something even more extraordinary: trash service. Instead of burying your garbage in the yard, people in carriages would actually come and take it away.

Lina always made sure to wrap up her garbage nicely for the trash men; sometimes she would use pretty ribbons she saved from gifts she'd been given.

"You saved everything," she says. "Every piece of string could be used for something else."

The Depression had hit and there was not much of anything to go around. Jerry was one of the lucky ones; he did not lose his job. But he took a pay cut of more than 50 percent. In 1941, just after the United States entered World War II, young Gerald went to work with the Merchant Marines. One day, a German U-boat off the coast of San Salvador torpedoed his ship. He was in the engine room and somehow managed to survive. He floated on a raft until he was rescued. Shortly afterward, he joined the army, setting mines along the Atlantic Coast to keep the enemy at bay.

War became a more urgent worry than money, which was virtually nonexistent during the war years. Even so, you would never expect a handout from the government. The very thought would have been unpatriotic; money was needed for the defense program. Like her neighbors, Lina raised a victory garden, both as a symbolic way of supporting the war effort and as a real way of putting food on the table. One summer Lina kept track of every bean and tomato in a little brown notebook; she wanted to know how much money she had saved by growing her own food. She was astounded to see that her harvest had netted the family a full twenty dollars.

Violet remembers it all, while Melissa listens in awe and young Rebecca of the MTV generation seems incredulous. Lina spots an antique doll on the other side of the room, and asks Violet for it. The doll's hair is long and red. "My mother made that for me," she says, running her fingers through the doll's curls. "And she used my own hair."

"You take care of it after Violet," she says to her granddaughter. "And after that, you take it," she instructs Rebecca, hoping that she, too, will cherish the paths women have known.

LONG ISLAND NATIVE LINA BEACON SITS IN THE BACKYARD OF HER HOME (p. 102). Before her marriage to Jerry, Lina spent her teenage years (p. 105) working at prestigious New York City department stores such as B. Altman and Lord & Taylor.

etta
moten barnett

Her Heart Keeps On Singing

Born 1901

As a little girl singing in a Texas church choir, Etta Moten could never have imagined herself one day appearing on the Hollywood screen. She could never have pictured herself becoming one of the first black women to perform at the White House. And she certainly never thought she'd star on Broadway in an opera that would become legendary.

"I just loved to sing," she says with a shrug. At ninety-six, Etta lives in a large Victorian on Chicago's South Side with her daughter Sue. She's dressed in purple velour, wears gold hoop earrings, and has a new manicure. She's surrounded by a lifetime of awards and honors and artifacts from her travels throughout Africa, but points out none of these. Instead, she calls attention to her father's college diploma.

"That's real sheepskin," she says, explaining that her father, a "free Negro," went to a Texas theological college and became a minister in the African Methodist Episcopal Church. "He knew Latin and Greek," she boasts. "He believed in education. That came first. You must be educated." He would even send Etta's mother to get her college degree. And as for Etta, an only child, the girl with the gorgeous contralto voice, she, too, should become a scholar, according to her father.

"But I wanted to get married," she says. Young Etta hadn't even finished high school when she announced her plans to wed her high school teacher and move with him to Oklahoma.

"My father was not happy," says Etta. In fact, he offered her $100 if she would reject the proposal. But Etta knew her mind. And her will was strong. It was the trait that would later become her power, helping her navigate her way through a country unkind to blacks and unfriendly to women. She believed in herself.

Etta had three daughters and stayed in the marriage for seven years before surrendering to the ugly truth. "He was a philanderer," she says. She couldn't take it anymore. There were no threats, no scenes. She simply packed up the children and moved back in with her parents, who were then living in Springfield, Missouri. She found herself a lawyer and got a divorce.

Her parents welcomed her home, and took care of the children during the week while Etta completed high school and college, returning home on the weekends to be with her girls. At the University of Kansas, she was one of about 150 black students out of almost 6,000. She studied voice and drama and graduated at thirty, then boarded a train for New York City. If singing was her gift, well, then sing she would. She was too naive to be intimidated by an entertainment industry that was not ready for a black woman in a starring role. She believed in herself.

On her way to New York, she stopped in Chicago and was introduced to the most remarkable man. He was a six-foot-four bachelor of forty-two. A newspaper man, and a kindred spirit.

Claude Barnett was a graduate of Alabama's Tuskegee Institute. He was a protégé of the college's founder and first president, Booker T. Washington, who preached self-help and black capitalism as a recipe for success. In 1919 Barnett started the Associated Negro Press, a wire service for the nation's black newspapers. It helped black America get to know itself. It brought feature stories, essays, poetry, and book and music reviews to a community that had once had little more to read about itself than news of lynchings.

Barnett had read about the talented Etta Moten in a newspaper that used his wire service. He was intrigued by this brazen girl who thought she could just hop a train and become a Broadway star. He said to her, "What makes you think you can make it in New York?"

"Because I'm good," she answered.

"And that's when we hit it off," she recalls. He wrote letters of introduction for her to prominent people in New York.

ETTA MOTEN BARNETT AT HOME, SURROUNDED BY THE AFRICAN ART she collected during trips taken with husband Claude (p. 106), and in a studio shot from the 1930s (p. 107). The song she sang in the film *Gold Diggers of 1933*, "My Forgotten Man," became a favorite of President Franklin Roosevelt's. Etta in her pre-Broadway days, in a promotional photo for a college radio show (p. 108). Etta now shares her Chicago home with her daughter Sue (*background*, p. 111).

In Harlem in the 1930s cabarets were thriving places, but often with "white patrons only" policies. And most black entertainers had to play for low pay for years in all-black clubs—which were often dirty, dim, ramshackle places—before being accepted by the more prestigious white clubs. But Etta beat the odds and appeared on Broadway in *Fast and Furious* within months of her arrival. Her second show, *Zombie,* evolved into a national tour that eventually brought her back to Chicago, where Claude Barnett again was waiting.

"And that's when Mr. Hardball Newspaper Man got to be Mr. Stage-Door Johnny," she says. The singer had captured Barnett's heart; he would do anything for her. He offered to introduce her to the movers and shakers he knew in Hollywood. Soon she was meeting with the managers of MGM, RKO, and Warner Brothers studios. Soon, in *Ladies of the Big House,* she was dubbing songs for Barbara Stanwyck and other stars.

"But you're not supposed to know that," she says, smiling. Etta's name did not appear in the credits.

"That was the business," she says. "You picked up your check and left." The jobs paid about $100 each.

In those early films black women appeared only as maids, servants, jolly overweight nannies. Etta broke out of those stereotypes in *Gold Diggers of 1933,* in which she played a beautiful widow. Reviewers called her "the new Negro woman." The song she sang—"My Forgotten Man"—became one of President Franklin D. Roosevelt's favorites. He invited Etta to the White House to sing it to him on his birthday.

Next she appeared in *Flying Down to Rio,* which paired Fred Astaire and Ginger Rogers for the first time. In it Etta sang "The Carioca," which was nominated for an Academy Award. The picture was released in 1933, and a year later she moved to Chicago, married Claude Barnett, and then brought her daughters, now young adolescents, to live with them.

"And that was the beginning of a very long and very wonderful love affair," she says.

Etta went on to sing and to bring down the house at Harlem's Apollo Theater. She remembers the day she met George Gershwin. He had just finished writing *Porgy and Bess.*

"He said, 'This is my first opera. This is my opera dream,'" she recalls. "And he said, 'You're my Bess. You've got to be!'" But he had written the part for a soprano. And Etta was a contralto. She tried to convince him that a low voice was more suited to Bess's character. He tried to convince her to learn to sing higher. The two could not agree and parted friends.

Porgy and Bess opened on Broadway in 1935. After star Anne Browne left the show in 1942, Etta took over and played Bess to critical acclaim. But the world was not entirely ready for black stars. Etta remembers having to find a room at the "colored" YWCA while her wardrobe mistress, a white woman, was put up in the best hotel.

Etta and Claude made their first trip to Africa in 1947, and over the next two decades they traveled extensively throughout the continent. They brought back a lot more than just Moroccan rugs and ivory sculptures for their home. They brought back stories about African leaders and culture for the Associated Negro Press. They brought back seeds of African-American pride.

Claude Barnett died in 1968, at seventy-three. He lived to see black journalists get jobs at mainstream newspapers.

Etta Moten has not performed publicly for nearly twenty-five years. "My voice," she says. "It just wore out." It happened while she was playing Bess. "I did it for too long." She says this with a sadness that is palpable, then looks at her daughter. "Could we listen to the tape?" she asks. Sue leads her mother to the kitchen, pushes a button on a portable recorder.

And out comes Etta in her prime. "Chasing Shadows," she sings. Her voice is thick, low, haunting. It's a recording from her radio program in the 1950s, *I Remember When.*

Etta, at ninety-six, listens, closes her eyes, breathes in deeply, then out. "'Chasing shadows / Chasing love dreams in vain / While my heart keeps on singing / Just a lonely refrain.'"

beatrice wood

Breaking the Mold

———

Born 1893

"What great women artists do we know who have been happily married?"
asks famed ceramicist Beatrice Wood, 105. She believes her own unhappiness—at
least when it comes to men—is the main reason she achieved success as an artist.

"Oh, now don't get started with sex and all of that," warns her manager of
twenty-two years, Ram Singh.

She looks at him, rolls her eyes. "You're a big stink," she says.

"Of course," he says. "I'm a man, right?"

A self-described flirt, she attributes her longevity to young men and chocolate.
Over her bed she has postcards of men in thongs. She ends her 1986 autobiography,
I Shock Myself, with this thought: "In a way, my life has been an upside-down experi-
ence. I never made love to the men I married, and I did not marry the men I loved.
I do not know if that makes me a good girl gone bad, or a bad girl gone good."

Beatrice Wood is said to be the last surviving member of the New York Dada circle, founders of a post–World War I movement that defied artistic conventions and

ushered in the era of modern art. "The Mama of Dada," they called her in a recent nationally touring eighty-year retrospective of her drawings, pottery, and saucy figurative sculptures.

"No, I am not the Mama of Dada," she says, seated in her home in Ojai, California, wearing her trademark hot-pink sari, pounds of silver jewelry from India, and her hair in a thick braid. "I was just in love with two of the men."

The two were painter Marcel Duchamp (*Nude Descending a Staircase*) and novelist Henri-Pierre Roche (*Jules et Jim,* the famous ménage à trois novel made into a popular film by François Truffaut).

She met them as a young woman dizzy for a Bohemian lifestyle, having fled her parents' strict upbringing. Born in San Francisco, she was raised in New York by governesses and sent away to boarding schools. "My mother was very interested in society, very elegant; she loved beautiful clothes, all that," she says. "And I remember she made me have a debut, which young girls were into years ago. I was in line with all these beautiful girls, one, two, three, everything very formal. And I left the line, went into the bathroom, locked the door, and wept.

"I was much more interested in art, literature, human relationships than in one's call to society. I was just born with that. And she couldn't change me. It was a great disappointment to her."

At nineteen, Beatrice fled to Paris, studied acting with teachers from the Comédie-Française, and once peeked through the hedges and saw Monet painting in his garden at Giverny. "There was enough space between the branches to see," she says. "I didn't intrude. I just watched."

With the outbreak of World War I, she returned to New York, acted in a repertory company, and met Duchamp at a cabaret. "And the fuel was in the fire immediately," she says. He showed her his drawings. "And I said to him, 'Oh, anybody can do those scrawls.' And he said, 'Okay, let's see you try it.' He said, 'Come to my studio.'"

"And that's when the fuel *really* went into the fire," says Singh.

"Yes," she says.

"Or, that's when you decided to avail yourself of his facilities," he says.

She rolls her eyes again.

She was twenty-two, in love, and she was drawing pictures, being schooled in the fundamentals of modern art. "Duchamp would look at my drawings and say, 'Good . . . bad . . . good . . . good . . . bad . . . bad.' And it became a part of me to realize that he liked the things that were not conventional."

During this same time, she met Roche, with whom she also fell in love, a deeper love, the kind of love that would impact her for the rest of her life. "I never believed in marriage," she says. "I've always said you can't make a law about love. But I was ready to accept the idea. I was brought up on fairy tales. And here I had a wonderful relationship. . . ."

She believed it would last forever.

But he dumped her for one of her best friends. And he told her about all the other women he had been sleeping with.

The devastation is still, at age 105, very much a part of her.

"I was brought up on fairy tales!" she repeats. "It was very hard for me to find out that life was not a fairy tale. I was twenty-two. And the prince in my life who appeared, suddenly all the toes fell off him. It was very, very rough for me."

The void in her heart is, she says, the source of her art. "If one is a really creative person, and has no man onto whom one can spill the creativity, one goes into something. It happened with me to be art." (She married twice after the Roche disaster, but neither marriage had anything to do with love. The first was to get free of her mother, and the second was to qualify for disaster relief after her home was destroyed in a California flood.)

In 1928 she headed west, leaving behind the vestiges of her Edwardian upbringing. A few years later, she enrolled in a ceramics class at Hollywood High School so she could

---

WEARING ONE OF HER TRADEMARK SARIS, CERAMICIST BEATRICE WOOD LOUNGES at home with her cat (p. 113). A member of the New York Dada circle, she relaxes with Francis Picabia and painter Marcel Duchamp, one of the loves of her life, in 1917 (p. 115). Beatrice and her manager of twenty-two years, Ram Singh, reminisce about old times in their Ojai, California, home (pp. 116–117).

make a teapot to match six antique lusterwear plates she had bought in Holland. She was forty years old when she discovered the passion that would change her life: clay.

On her fifty-fifth birthday she discovered the town of Ojai, two and a half hours north of Los Angeles. "Ojai was the pot of gold at the end of a long, obstacle-strewn rainbow," she writes in her autobiography. "From the moment I arrived on March 3, 1948, time ceased."

She has lived beneath the protective shadow of the Topa-Topa Mountain ever since. In 1961 she took the first of numerous trips to India, a source of much of her inspiration. "I saw all these women in saris, and men, old men with funny hairdos. I was in love with the country. Pictorially, it was wonderful." She has worn nothing but saris since that trip. And it was then that she met Singh, who moved into her spare bedroom and became her manager.

Up until a few years ago, she did a full day's work, rising at six-thirty and running in her pajamas to her kiln to see what surprises awaited. Her pots and sculptures would go on to be featured in the Smithsonian, the Metropolitan Museum of Art in New York, and other international museums.

The themes of her figurative work almost always involve a joke or a jab about the battle of the sexes. *Men with Wives* is a sculpture depicting couples sitting around a table, the men clearly bored. In *Marriage* a man and a woman are seated close to each other, but he's sipping coffee, looking away, ready to make a quick exit.

None of these works would exist, she insists, if she had been happily married. She would not have been an artist. "I would have put all my energy into trying to keep the man from other women," she says. "Which a wife has to do."

She's beginning to think that women should forgive men, though, for their infidelities. "It's very easy for men to get attracted, and it may mean nothing. Nothing. Oh, I don't know . . ."

"Are you willing to let this go, then?" asks Singh. "Are you willing to accept human weakness or will you still throw these men out on their ears?"

"It's been so long since I've been tempted," she says. "It's hard to answer."

Beatrice Wood once summed up her work and life this way: "When the bowl that was my heart was broken, laughter fell out."

FRIEDA MAY HARDIN

A Woman Goes to War

Born 1896

The bulletin boards in the nursing-home section of northern California's Livermore VA Hospital are plastered with newspaper articles and photos of its current star, Frieda May Hardin, 101. She's one of the few women residents here, and the only female World War I veteran. The articles tell of Frieda's show-stopping speech at the recent dedication of the Women in Military Service for America Memorial in Washington, D.C.—a permanent reminder of women's contributions to the nation's defense.

"Yeah, I went over big," she says, sitting on her bed in her small room. "And you know, I met the high-ups," she says, referring to Vice President Al Gore and Tipper Gore. "All this because of the navy," she says. "I am so proud I was in the navy."

The idea came to her at age twenty-two—quite without warning. Frieda was a shoe-factory worker in Portsmouth, Ohio, where she lived with her overprotective mother, and her father, who worked in a flour mill and whom Frieda adored. One Saturday night at dinner, her father remarked on the oddest thing he had read that day in the newspaper:

"They're taking women in the navy now," he said. It was 1918 and the United States had entered World War I a year earlier and was experiencing manpower shortages. The secretary of the navy had proposed a novel solution: Enlist women for stateside duty so that sailors could be released for sea duty.

Frieda listened to her parents discuss the idea of women joining the armed forces. Her father was interested, her mother disdainful. This was not a proper place for women, her mother said. Women were, after all, not even allowed to vote.

"The navy!" Frieda said to her parents. "I think that's for me!" She surprised even herself with her enthusiasm for the idea. She had never had any particular urge to serve her country. Perhaps this was simply a way to break free from her mother. Perhaps it was her ticket out of the drudgery of factory work.

Or perhaps it was the novelty of the idea. Women had served in the U.S. armed forces since colonial times—sometimes disguised as men, sometimes accompanying their soldier husbands to war and serving as cooks and seamstresses—and had only became quasiofficial members of the American military in 1901 with the creation of the army nurse corps, followed by the navy nurse corps in 1908. Both corps were auxiliaries of their services, however, and their female members did not receive benefits equal to those of men.

It was quite an extraordinary thing, then, to see women recruited into the *real* navy, the same one that men joined.

The navy became the first of the services to recruit women, enlisting almost twelve thousand over the course of the war, beginning in 1917. These women were given the title yeoman (F) and were paid at the same rate as male yeoman. The marine corps followed, enlisting 305 women shortly before the end of the war.

Frieda went down to the recruiting station first thing Monday morning. She enlisted, then called her mother. "Mama, I just joined the navy!" she said.

Her mother said, "Frieda, you come right home."

Frieda obeyed. She walked in the door and saw that her mother had brought in reinforcements: Frieda's aunt. "And they both landed on me roughshod," says Frieda. "Oh, they gave me a terrible going over. You'd think I'd committed a crime."

Her mother marched Frieda back down to the recruiting office. "This girl is not going into the navy!" she said.

"Why?" asked the recruiting officer.

"Um," her mother said, thinking about that for a moment. She couldn't actually come up with a reason. "Because," she finally blurted out, "she hasn't got her father's consent."

"And so the recruiter turned to me and he said, 'You go home and talk to your father about it and come back tomorrow.' And so we went home. And when we mentioned it to Daddy he said, 'Well, let her go.' And that settled it for Mama."

Frieda was sent on active duty to Norfolk, Virginia, where she was a yeoman third class (F). Her job was strictly clerical: She checked dock receipts in the freight office. She was paid $41 a month, plus $2 for living expenses. There was no housing for women, so she lived in a boardinghouse in town. In six months the war was over, and she was released from duty.

"And my mother started urging me to come home, so I did," she recalls. Before long she was answering an ad in the paper for a man looking for a wife. She met William Kirsten, a chef in a lumber camp near Seattle, Washington, who was twenty years her senior. Within about a week they were married. The couple had four children, and Frieda was miserably unhappy. "I couldn't take any more of him," she says. "He was too brutal to me. But he was good to the children. He was awfully good to the children."

She left one night while he was cooking dinner. She took her youngest child, Warren, just six, and left the older three in his care.

She moved back to her parents' home, and continued searching for happiness. She married three more times in her life, the last time to Robert Hardin, when she was in her eighties.

"I had two bad husbands and two good ones," she says. "The last two were good." She outlived both of them.

Frieda reunited with the rest of her children in the 1950s, all of whom accepted her with open arms, and are involved in Frieda's life today. Three of them, Warren, Mary, and Jerald, accompanied her to Washington, D.C.,

"I AM SO PROUD I WAS IN THE NAVY," SAYS WORLD WAR I VETERAN Frieda May Hardin, now living in California's Livermore VA Hospital (p. 118). In 1918 the navy announced it was looking for women for stateside duty—Frieda enlisted two days later (p. 121).

in October 1997 to the dedication of the Women in Military Service for America Memorial.

"In my one hundred and one years of living," Frieda said to the crowd of some thirty thousand people, "I have observed many wonderful achievements, but none as important or as meaningful as the progress of women in taking their rightful place in society."

So much had happened for women in the armed forces since that day in 1918 when Frieda defied her mother's wishes to join the navy. Most of the advances had occurred in the latter half of the century, following the Women's Armed Services Integration Act of 1948, which President Truman signed into law. The law gave women permanent status in the army, navy, air force, and marine corps. No longer would special women's "components" be formed merely for the duration of military emergencies. Women were now bona fide members of the regular armed forces and the reserves, subject to military authority and entitled to veterans' benefits.

In 1968 the air force promoted the first woman to colonel. In 1970 the army promoted the first woman to brigadier general. In 1973 six navy women earned military pilots' wings. In 1980 the first group of women graduated from the service academies and entered active duty. In 1988 America got its first female navy astronaut. In the early 1990s nearly all legal restrictions against women in combat were lifted by Congress. By mid-1995 women were serving as part of mixed-sex crews on navy combat ships and women pilots were flying combat aircraft.

Women currently account for about 12 percent of the total military force in America. To date, nearly 2 million women have served in the defense of the United States.

"It's not likely that I will be meeting with you again," said Frieda, standing at the podium that day. "So I bid each of you a fond farewell. God bless the United States Navy, and God Bless America."

caroline
schaffner

Always Leave Them Laughing

Born 1901

NEIL AND CAROLINE
SCHAFFNER PLAYERS

FEATURING

TOBY AND SUSIE

WCAZ

Stars of
"TOBY'S COCKEYED NOOZ"
Radio's Comedy Sensation

THE

SHOW

WITH A

MILLION

FRIENDS

STAGE AND

RADIO

STARS

IN

PERSON

TOBY AND SUSIE in 1937

If she learned nothing else in her forty years of performing in tent shows throughout the Midwest, Caroline Schaffner learned to keep her audience amused. At ninety-six, she has not let go of the goal.

"Welcome," she says, opening the door of her home in Mount Pleasant, Iowa, where she lives alone. "Do you want something to eat? Here, put your coat here. Okay, now this is the living room. And turn on a couple of the lights. Because I want to show you my collection of cups and saucers. There. Isn't that something? Quite a choice collection. Okay, I'm going to sit down. Look around because this is where I've lived for the past twenty-four years."

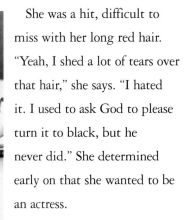

She has a way of directing the conversation.

"Now," she says, "do you, by any chance, have any conception of what it is when I talk about a tent show? It was the only live entertainment for people in rural areas. Okay, sit back and I'll tell you about it. But then I have to go to the hairdresser."

Tent shows are part of the history of repertory theater in America. Beginning in the 1850s, troupes of performers traveled rural America entertaining audiences with week-long stands of Broadway hits, adapted classics, and other standard plays. At first these performances would appear in the town's opera houses—which would become unbearably hot in the summers. And so they were moved outside, under enormous tents that the actors themselves would pitch in town after town. As opera houses were converted into movie houses, live theater was performed almost exclusively under tents. By 1920 there were some four hundred tent theater organizations scattered around the United States.

Caroline was part of one of the most enduring of all the tent-show companies, The Schaffner Players.

She and her husband, Neil, were the managers and stars.

Caroline Helen Hannah was born in Orange, Texas, the only child of a lumberman and his wife. Her grandfather, an Irish immigrant, had founded the town's Presbyterian church. "And it was there that I got my first experience singing before an audience," she says.

She was a hit, difficult to miss with her long red hair. "Yeah, I shed a lot of tears over that hair," she says. "I hated it. I used to ask God to please turn it to black, but he never did." She determined early on that she wanted to be an actress.

When she was twenty-three she had a part in the chorus line with a musical comedy company called Al Russell and His Sizzling Cuties, which performed "tab shows," short live acts between movies during the days of silent films.

Neil Schaffner, a tent-theater manager who was in town with his own production, was in the audience one night. He couldn't keep his eyes off the little redhead at the end of the chorus line. After the show, he made a beeline backstage and introduced himself to her.

Did she fall immediately in love with him?

"I fell in love with the job offer," she says. "I was very ambitious for show business." Neil told her about his theater

CAROLINE, RELAXING IN HER IOWA LIVING ROOM TODAY (P. 122) AND BEAMING in a 1926 publicity shot (p. 123). Caroline and Neil Schaffner brought their acts to radio in 1935, broadcasting "Toby's Cockeyed Nooz" in 1936 (*top*, p. 124) and "Bug Tussel News," in 1937 and 1938 (*background*, p. 124). Son Rome Lee, born in 1926, later joined his parents' tent shows (*bottom*, p. 124). After Neil's death in 1969, Caroline established the Theater Museum of Repertoire Americana, which she continues to maintain. The Schaffners' most popular plays involved Neil as Toby and Caroline as Susie (p. 127).

company, and within a year Caroline was touring with him for $30 a week. Gradually, she and Neil fell in love. They would go for dinner every night after shows, until one night Neil told her that, for the business's sake, he might have to dine with different women on some occasions.

That stopped her cold. "If I am not going to be all of it," she told him, "I'm not going to be in it at all. You can just make up your mind which you prefer."

They were married two months later, in 1925. A year after that they had a son who traveled with them and performed in the shows. Caroline was in charge of hiring the actors, anywhere from ten to twenty-five a season. "The thing that got you your job was how many trunks of wardrobe you could furnish," she says. Plus, you needed a "specialty," the ability to dance or juggle or whistle. A young Clark Gable got fired from a tent-theater troupe because he did not have a specialty. Bob Hope and Red Skelton also got their starts in tent repertoire.

Caroline and Neil went on to write, direct, and act in original plays for nearly four decades, delighting audiences with their most popular characters, Toby, a country bumpkin who would prove to be wise, and his girlfriend, Susie.

"You had to please the public," she says. "They liked romantic things, and comedies, and a little lesson. Right always prevailed over wrong. That's what they believed, and that's what you gave them. My husband understood this. And whenever he had written a new play, he would stand in the wings watching, not the stage but the audience. 'Are they being entertained?' 'Are they listening?' 'Are they interested?' If not, Neil would stay up half the night rewriting the scenes."

He was a clever businessman who managed to keep his company alive against all the odds: first the Depression, and then what could have been the real killer, radio.

During the Depression he came up with clever marketing schemes. He worked out deals with shop owners whose patrons were too deeply in debt to afford theater tickets. He advertised a free season pass to The Schaffner Players for every five dollars paid on a shopkeeper's overdue bill.

In exchange, he collected a dollar from the shopkeeper for every ticket given away. In other towns he worked deals with telephone offices. In return for a couple of season passes for the operators, he got on the phone and called all of the rural party lines at once. He made his pitch for the show, offering ladies free admission if they came with a paying husband.

"The generation today," says Caroline, "no matter what words you use, cannot conceive of what it was like during the Depression. They have no idea how tough times were."

When radio came in—entertainment you could get in your very own home—many tent theater companies went out of business. Neil Schaffner's idea was to use radio as a friend rather than a foe. In 1935 the Schaffners began performing a comedy act on an Illinois radio station. From 1936 to 1938 they had a weekly act on the NBC *Barn Dance* show out of Chicago. They continued to take their tent show on the road every summer and were able to capitalize on the success of their radio personalities.

It wasn't until 1962, due to Neil Schaffner's ailing health, that The Schaffner Players performed their farewell tour. Neil died in 1969. His final words to his wife were, "Caroline, establish a museum."

She has devoted the rest of her life to the task.

In 1973 the Theater Museum of Repertoire Americana opened in Mt. Pleasant, Iowa. Caroline moved to her present home on a shady street near the museum so she could oversee its operations. When the museum hosted its first festival of Schaffner plays recently, Caroline showed up every night as its honored guest. People flocked for her autograph, for one final glimpse of the family that had brought live entertainment to rural communities of the Midwest.

She loved seeing her audience again. She watched them, as Neil once did, from the sidelines. A lot had changed since her days of performing onstage, but a lot of things had stayed the same. "People like the romantic things," she says. "And comedy, and a little lesson. They like when right prevails over wrong."

1946 More marriages take place than in any other year, contributing to the baby boom.

1947 The Army-Navy Nurse Act creates permanent commissions for military nurses. Margaret Wise Brown writes *Goodnight Moon*. The transistor is invented.

1948 The Marshall Plan offers billions of dollars in aid to European countries. Israel is established. The World Health Organization is created. The Women's Armed Services Integration Act gives women regular military status, although limits are put on top rank and number of top officers. Stalin blockades West Berlin. Apartheid begins to take hold in South Africa.

1949 The Soviets successfully test their atomic bomb. The North Atlantic Treaty Organization (NATO) is established. Harvard Law School decides to admit women. Almost 30 percent of all women work, representing about 25 percent of the workforce.

1950 Senator McCarthy charges that communists have infiltrated the Department of State. Julius and Ethel Rosenberg are arrested for selling atomic secrets to the Soviets; they will later be found guilty and put to death. The Korean War begins. The U.S. Census Bureau recognizes a woman's right to continue to use her maiden name after marriage.

1951 *I Love Lucy* starring Lucille Ball airs on CBS. Marion Donovan invents a disposable diaper, which she manufactures herself because no companies are interested. She will later sell her business for $1 million.

1952 The Allied military occupation of Japan ends. The United States tests the first hydrogen bomb.

1953 James Dewey Watson and Francis Crick propose their model of DNA. Mount Everest is successfully scaled. The Korean War ends. Legislation is enacted by Congress to permit the immigration of 500,000 Eastern Europeans driven from their homes as a result of political or racial persecution. The Academy Awards are televised for the first time.

1954 The Supreme Court rules, in *Brown v. Board of Education*, that racially segregated schools are unconstitutional. Elvis Presley releases his first hit, "That's All Right." Some color television transmission begins. Jonas Salk's polio vaccine is proven safe and effective. The first succesful kidney transplant is performed. The TV dinner is introduced.

1955 Rosa Parks is arrested for refusing to give up her seat on a bus to a white man. The Montgomery bus boycott will last for more than a year. Disneyland opens in California.

1956 The Highway Trust Fund is created, accelerating the construction of the interstate highway system. Grace Kelly is married to Prince Rainier II of Monaco. *The Diary of Anne Frank* wins both a Tony and a Pulitzer. Rock Hudson receives a Best Actor nomination for his performance in *Giant*.

1957 The Soviet Union launches *Sputnik*. The school board of Little Rock, Arkansas, announces it will racially integrate the school system.

1958 NASA is created, and the first U.S. satellite, *Explorer 1*, is launched. The hula hoop is introduced.

1959 Castro assumes power in Cuba. The Barbie doll is introduced by Ruth Handler, cofounder of Mattel toy company. NASA begins recruiting for astronauts. Pantyhose enter the marketplace.

1960 The Food and Drug Administration approves birth control pills. John F. Kennedy and Richard Nixon appear in the first televised U.S. presidential debate. About 35 percent of all women work. They average 60 cents for every dollar earned by men.

1961 Yuri Gagarin, a Soviet cosmonaut, is the first person in space. Almost a month later, American Alan Shepard becomes the second. The Peace Corps is created. The Berlin Wall is built. President Kennedy creates the President's Commission on the Status of Women; it's chaired by Eleanor Roosevelt. Roger Maris hits sixty-one home runs in one season, taking the record from Babe Ruth.

1962 John Glenn Jr. makes the first U.S. manned orbital flight around the Earth. Bette Davis and Joan Crawford star in *Whatever Happened to Baby Jane?* Nelson Mandela, an activist for South African black civil rights, is arrested and imprisoned. Helen Gurley Brown's *Sex and the Single Girl* is published.

1963 The President's Commission on the Status of Women issues a report documenting discrimination against women in virtually every area of American life. The Equal Pay Act is an amendment to the Fair Labor Standards Act that prohibits wage discrimination based on sex. Martin Luther King Jr. leads the March on Washington. John F. Kennedy is assassinated in Dallas. The United States, Soviet Union, and United Kingdom agree to the Limited Nuclear Test-Ban Treaty. Valium is released.

1964 The Civil Rights Act is passed, prohibiting discrimination in employment on the basis of race, creed, national origin, or sex. The government-sponsored Head Start program is launched to help prepare children of low-income families for school. The Supremes have their first of twelve number one hits with "Where Did Our Love Go?" Seventy-three million people watch the Beatles on the *Ed Sullivan Show*.

1965 President Johnson orders federal agencies and contractors to take "affirmative action" in overcoming employment discrimination. The Supreme Court rules that laws prohibiting the use of birth control are unconstitutional. The United States enters the Vietnam War. Malcolm X is assassinated.

1966 The National Organization for Women (NOW) is founded by Betty Friedan to function as a civil rights organization for women. Jacqueline Susann's *The Valley of the Dolls* becomes a bestseller.

1967 NOW holds its first national conference and resurrects the fight for the Equal Rights Amendment. Race riots break out in Newark, New Jersey, and Detroit, Michigan. Janis Joplin releases "Ball and Chain" and becomes the first female rock superstar.

1968 Reverend Martin Luther King Jr. and Senator Robert Kennedy are both assassinated. Affirmative action is expanded to include women. New York City institutes the first 911 emergency telephone system in the United States. The motion picture industry introduces a ratings system. Shirley Temple Black is appointed by President Nixon as a U.S. representative at the United Nations.

1969 Neil Armstrong is the first person to step on the moon. U.S. military strength in South Vietnam peaks at over 550,000. Four hundred thousand attend the Woodstock music festival. California legalizes abortion. Yale University admits its first female undergraduates. *Sesame Street* debuts. California adopts the nation's first "no fault" divorce law.

1970 Four students are killed and nine wounded when National Guard troops fire into a crowd of antiwar protesters at Ohio's Kent State University. Close to 44 percent of all women work, averaging 59 cents for every dollar earned by men. *The Mary Tyler Moore Show* premieres.